Traveling
Toward
Sunrise

Books by Mrs. Cowman—

Streams in the Desert—1
    formerly titled *Streams in the Desert*

Streams in the Desert—2
    formerly titled *Streams in the Desert, Volume 2*

Springs in the Valley
    formerly titled *Springs in the Desert—3*

Traveling Toward Sunrise
    formerly titled *Springs in the Desert—4*

Words of Comfort and Cheer
    formerly titled *Springs in the Desert—5*

Streams in the Desert Sampler

Mountain Trailways for Youth

Traveling Toward Sunrise

Mrs. Charles Cowman

Zondervan Publishing House
Grand Rapids, Michigan

Traveling Toward Sunrise
Copyright © 1944, 1972 by Mrs. Charles E. Cowman

Daybreak Books are published by the
Zondervan Publishing House
1415 Lake Drive, S.E.,
Grand Rapids, Michigan 49506

Library of Congress Cataloging-in-Publication Data

Cowman, Charles E., Mrs., 1870–1960.
    Traveling towards sunrise.

    "Daybreak Books."
    1. Devotional calendars.   I. Title.
BV4811.C684   1988   242'.2   88-20858
ISBN 0-310-35390-4

Traveling Toward Sunrise formerly appeared as *Streams in the
Desert—4.*

Printed in the United States of America

88 89 90 91 92 93 / AK / 30 29 28 27 26

To Miss Lydia Bemmels, R.N.,
whose devotion, affection and companionship
have been such an inexpressible blessing
to me during the past twenty-eight years,
I lovingly dedicate this volume.

To Mr. Floyd W. Thatcher,
whose strong encouragement, invaluable advice,
and unique business ability have made possible
the publishing of this book,
I owe an immeasurable debt of gratitude.

To my God-given, dearly beloved friend,
Mrs. Raymond L. Cramer,
without whose literary efficiency
and untiring faithfulness to the task,
this volume could not have been produced,
I offer my very sincere and heartfelt thanks.

FOREWORD

Since the birth of STREAMS IN THE DESERT a quarter of a century ago, the multitude of letters from its readers has brought much joy to my heart and deepened the conviction that a companion volume to STREAMS IN THE DESERT should be written.

Throughout the years I have gathered bits of poetry and prose which have enriched my life. These I have longed to share with you, my fellow travelers, at all stages of your journey along the pilgrim road.

The preparation of this volume, with its many details has been a delightful experience and long, happy hours have been spent in the arranging of the materials. The task has been done out of love to you and to my Lord.

If through His blessing, the journey toward sunrise is made happier and easier for you, His beloved children, I shall feel that my prayers have been answered.

Mrs. Charles E. Cowman.

The children of Israel journeyed . . . from the wilderness . . . toward the sunrising (Num. 21:11).

Traveling in the wilderness toward the sunrising! The very words have poetry in them. These travelers were time's valiant great hearts. They were journeying on the star road making their way through an uninspiring land, a desert waste, upheld by hope of a glorious new day, a tomorrow morning, when night with its darkness and shadows would be left far behind. Travelers whose hopes were fixed on what was before and beyond; men of faith who followed the gleam loyally, right through to the very end; road-makers, presenting an unparalleled example of courage and bravery; men of vision, always looking ahead, never behind.

What an inspiring, challenging thought as we enter into the new year and begin our journey, traveling toward sunrise. Let us begin by filling the air with songs of rejoicing, with songs not sighs, for we are wayfarers of the infinite, traveling to the land where dawns are begotten and glory has its dwelling place, where life begins, not ends, and where there is eternal springtime.

> And I said to the man who stood at the gate of the year,
> "Give me a light that I may tread safely into the
>   unknown!"
> And he replied:
> "Go out into the darkness and put your hand into the
>   Hand of God.
> That shall be to you better than light and safer than a
>   known way."
> So I went forth, and finding the Hand of God, trod gladly
>   into the night.
> And He led me toward the hills and the breaking of day
>   in the lone East.   *M. Louise Haskins.*

Surrounded then as we are by these serried ranks of witnesses, let us strip off everything that hinders, as well as the sin which dogs our feet and let us run the race that we have to run with patience (Heb. 12:1—Phillips' Trans.).

"From whence came this vast multitude and who are they?" might well have been the question asked by the great cloud of witnesses who from their battlements on high are looking down upon the travelers, watching the race that they are running.

These are the pioneers of this generation. They are way-worn, their garments travel-stained, their feeble steps indicating weariness, their faces bearing deep furrowed lines of suffering.

Among this vast company are those who are just beginning the journey, in the morning of life, some who have attained their life's noonday, others who are well into the midafternoon, a large number who have reached the autumn of life and a far greater number who are nearing the eventide.

All have left the wilderness and started on a wonderful journey, declaring plainly that they are seeking a country where the sun never sets, the leaves never fade. They have pitched their tents toward the sunrising—the timeless and ageless life—their Fatherland.

> God's road is all uphill
>   But do not tire;
> Rejoice that we may still
>   Keep climbing higher.

Arthur Guiterman.

John 13:2-20

Behold I am with thee and will keep thee in all places whither thou goest . . . for I will not leave thee, until I have done that which I have spoken to thee of (Gen. 28:15).

It is very delightful and encouraging to enter upon the year before us with the consciousness that infinite wisdom, love and power have covered the coming months and days with the assurance of every needed blessing. The saddest thing about the lives of the unsaved, is that they are uncovenanted lives. Nothing is safe or sure. Everything is at their own risk. But for us, divine love has guaranteed all future needs. There is a way in which this is not only generally true as a matter of course, but may be made very special and definite by an act of consecration and faith. Many of the most useful and honored of God's servants have found it an unspeakable blessing to enter into a definite covenant with their heavenly Father, and record it, and look back upon the past and see how God has kept His pledge.

It is not so much what we promise as what we take and let Him undertake. *Shall we go into a covenanted year and hear him say to us: "Behold I am with thee and will keep thee."*

Psalm 119:65-72
The Bible is meant for daily use:
not cake for special occasions

And . . . Jesus himself drew near and went with them (Luke 24:15).

The Berkeley Version of this verse reads, "Jesus himself caught up with them and walked along." Another version, "He himself shall be with them traveling the road." The road often leads through green pastures, and beside the still waters, more often through long valleys, shadowless and deep, over mountains unscalable; but let us ask no question concerning the road as we journey, for the road leads Home and He Himself is with us.

A special cause for thankfulness lies in the fact that the chosen path never proves to be a blind alley. The road is a thoroughfare. A Red Sea may confront the travelers, but only to reveal a way through. The wayfarer's Pathfinder made the passage through and will keep it clear until the last traveler is safely over.

We are not a divided company, we are roadmates. Together is the watchword of this generation. We travel together in company with our risen Lord. Sharing common joys and sorrows, enjoying each other's experiences and discoveries, the travelers go from company to company until the last bend in the road brings them into the midst of the innumerable company already at Home.

Dear Companion of our journeyings, help us to walk so close beside Thee in the darkness of the night that when the dawn breaks and the shadows flee, we may enter into the full radiance of thy glory and the life everlasting. Amen.

2 cor. 9:6-15
when you give to God you gain

He that chooseth as his permanent abode the secret place of the Most High shall always be in touch with the Almightiness of God (Psalm 91:1—Modern Trans.).

J esus," said S. D. Gordon, "was always conscious of His Father's presence and the most natural thing was to speak to Him. They were always within speaking distance, and always on speaking terms."

So closely is the life of the road connected with the invisible goal that prayer has been established as a special means of communication between the two. Prayer is that preparation for the travelers' benefit so unique that it stands alone in the tale of their blessings. It is cooperation with God. In prayer we align ourselves to the purposes of God and He is able to do things through us that He could not do otherwise.

> Prayer is so simple;
> It is like quietly opening a door
> And slipping into the very presence of God.
> There in the stillness
> To listen to His voice,
> Perhaps to petition,
> Or only to listen;
> It matters not
> Just to be there
> In His presence
> Is prayer.

I have been young and now am old; yet have I not seen the righteous forsaken, nor his seed begging bread (Psalm 37:25).

When I came to the gate that is at the head of the way, the Lord of that place gave me such things that were necessary for my journey and bade me hope to the end. *Pilgrim's Progress.*

Every traveler setting out on a journey naturally wonders, "What is the distance? Am I equal to it? How shall I fare on the road?"

Perpetual strength to walk in God's way is found to be the traveler's birthright. His sandals are proof against the roughest road and tender feet grown weary with the long journey shall be carried in His strong arms.

> Upon the threshold of another year
>   We stand again.
> We know not what of gladness and good cheer
>   Or grief or pain
> May visit us while journeying to its close.
>   In this we rest,
> God dealeth out in wisdom what He knows
>   For us is best.
>   *Thomas Wearing.*

want to focus on Gods leading and direction in the year 2001.

Blessed are they that dwell in thy house; they will be still praising thee (Psalm 84:4).

As well the singers as the players on instruments shall be there . . . (Psalm 87:7).

As soldiers beguile the weariness of a long march with cheerful songs of home, so in olden days the wayfarers bound for Jerusalem sang as they journeyed. The score of their music has long since been lost, yet every traveler to the Heavenly Jerusalem knows the melody by heart. It begins and ends on the note of love.

Had these singers then never found the road difficult? Was it never dark or cold or lonely? Indeed it was, but looking back they see that it was the King's road, the royal road and for it they are still praising.

> I am going on my journey glad with joy from dawn
>   to dark
> With the spirit of the morning and the carol of the lark,
> I am drinking of those fountains whence the healing
>   waters flow,
> And I hear Heaven's sweetest music as along my way
>   I go.
>
> And my heart is full of laughter, like the singing of
>   a psalm;
> And my sky behind bends blue above me, with its winds
>   of evening balm,
> And I know not any trouble; for I have the Tempest's King,
> To change my winter's fury to the gladness of the Spring.
>
> *Wm. A. Quayle.*

If any man will come after me, let him deny himself and take up his cross daily and follow me (Luke 9:23).

The crosses which we make for ourselves by over-anxiety as to the future are not Heaven-sent crosses. We tempt God by our false wisdom, seeking to forestall His arrangements, and struggling to supplement His Providence by our own provisions. The future is not ours. Let us shut our eyes to that which God hides from us in the hidden depths of His Wisdom. Let us worship without seeing.

The crosses actually laid upon us always bring their own special grace and consequent comfort with them; we see the hand of God when it is laid upon us. But the crosses wrought by anxious foreboding are altogether beyond God's dispensations; we meet them without the special grace adapted to the need—nay, rather in a faithless spirit, which precludes grace. So everything seems hard and unendurable; all seems dark, helpless and the soul finds nought save hopeless rebellion and death within. All this comes of not trusting to God and prying into His hidden ways. "Sufficient unto the day is the evil thereof," our Lord has said, and the evil of each day becomes good if we leave it to God.   *F. F.*

> I do not ask my cross to understand,
> My way to see;
> Better in the darkness just to feel Thy hand
> And follow Thee.   *Adelaide Procter.*

The Lord shall increase you more and more . . . (Psalm 115:14).

Thou standest on the threshold
   of days which are unknown,
Thou standest at the gateway of
   paths unmapped, unshown;
But God himself is with thee,
   thy Saviour, Keeper, Friend;
And He will not forsake thee nor
   leave thee to life's end.
Thou standest and thou askest:
   "What have the days in store?"
He answereth thee: "Blessing!"
   "Yea, blessing more and more."
What form that blessing taketh,
   thou mayest not yet know;
But blessing upon blessing He
   waiteth to bestow.

We never have to make provision for the whole journey, but merely for one step at a time.

In Jehovah my Lord have I taken up my shelter (Psalm 73:28—Spurrell).

It is the Christian alone who can make due preparation for the voyage of life. For him only is the channel charted and lighted. The Book of God gives him his sailing directions. In Christ he has a Pilot who knows the soundings, and who has never lost a ship.

I watch my Father's face as the storm approaches and seeing His smile as the cloud musters and gathers I am satisfied. Fear has no place since He safely dwells with me. All's safe when God is around.

> There's a Hand on the rudder that will not flinch.
>   There's no fear on the Pilot's face,
> As He guides the world like a boat in a storm,
>   Through the rocking sea of space.

When thou liest down, thou shalt not be afraid, yea thou shalt lie down and thy sleep shall be sweet (Prov. 3:24).

> God make my thoughts like little quiet sheep,
>   And keep them in Thy sight
> Through the dark hours, the dusk and dawn between,
> Guide them and guard them from the steep ravine,
>   And fold them in at night.
> Often they stray upon the moor of fear,
>   Lost on its rocky height;
> Oh, in Thy peaceful pastures let them sleep,
> Shepherd my thoughts like little quiet sheep,
>   And fold them in at night.   *Lady Irvine.*

Faith will not make the sun rise sooner, but it will make the night seem shorter.

Enter ye in at the strait gate . . . (Matt. 7:13).

Will the road you are traveling bring you to the place you hope to reach? On Barr's Trail up the slope of Pike's Peak, there is a place where the trail divides. One marker reads: "To the Summit"; the other, "To the Bottomless Pit." A step decides the goal. We too often do some shabby living and expect to reach nobleness. We take short cuts in morality and expect to develop character. The way we are living and the road we are traveling determine the kind of character we will have in the end.

The road that nations take decides the goal at which the world will arrive. The path of unrighteousness will not create a righteous world. Right ends do not justify wrong means, for wrong means bring us to wrong ends. To have a righteous world, we must do righteous deeds. He who chooses the beginning of a road chooses the place it leads to.

Those who live on the mountain top have a much longer day.

Apart to his disciples, he explained all (Mark 4:34—Englishman's Greek New Testament).

L ife is before us, not behind. This should be at once the crown of all our hopes for the future, and the one great lesson taught us by all the vicissitudes of life. The sorrows and the joys, the journeying and the rest, the temporary repose and the frequent struggles; all these should make us sure that there is an end which will interpret them all—to which they all point— for which they all prepare.

How often we think we see God's plans clearly from a mere glimpse at a part of it. To wait and trust is often the latest lesson we learn in life.

> This is my faith in Thee,
> Tall Christ of Galilee,
> Where'er I may be
>   Thou art before—
> Then on the dizzying trail
> Then on the shadowed gale,
>   Ever before.   *Robert Freeman*

We take our journey to and through eternity with Thee, O Christ, in jubilation and with tireless song. A song which shall not come to gloaming like the babe's call, but which shall endure for ages, like the singing of the angels in heavenly hills.

For we are made partakers of Christ, if we hold the beginning of our
confidence steadfast unto the end (Heb. 3:14).

The path was steep and snowy—the way was hard
      and cold,
The wind rushed fiercely at us like a wolf upon the fold;
We bit our lips and struggled in the terror of the blast.
And we blessed our staffs and wondered if the storm
      would soon be past.
Sometimes our feet slipped backward on the crusty ice
      and snow.
Sometimes we stumbled, helpless for the way was hard
      to go;
Sometimes we fell and falling we were sorry we had tried
To reach the mountain's summit and the hope within us
      died.

The path was steep and snowy—the way was hard
      and cold,
But we struggled ever forward, half afraid, no longer bold,
And with dogged perseverance, we pushed up the
      hidden trail,
And we seemed but children playing with the elements—
      too frail
To live long in the displeasure of the wind and hail
      and sleet,
And the snowy down-like blanket seemed a mammoth
      winding sheet . . .
And we almost started homeward with a weary broken
      sigh,
But we flinched and struggled forward 'neath the scorn
      that cleft the sky.

The path was steep and snowy—the way was hard
      and cold,
But at least we reached the summit, and it glittered with
      the gold
Of the sun that had been shining, with a perfect,
      glowing light
From behind the heavy storm clouds that had turned the
      day to night,
And standing on the summit, we looked down and tried
      to pray,
For we wished to thank the Father who had kept us on
      our way;

For the snow and sleet and windstorm were but trifles in
   the past,
And they made the sunshine brighter when we reached
   the top at last.   *Margaret Elizabeth Sangster.*

Life has a wonderful way of tapering majestically to its climax. It
narrows itself up toward its supremacies like a mountain rising to
its snow-capped summit in the skies.

Behold I have graven thee on the palms of my hands; thy walls are continually before me (Isa. 49:16).

A skeptic noticed a robin's nest in a gigantic elm and heard a still small voice saying, "If God spent a hundred years in creating a tree like that for a bird, He will surely take care of you."

God is so interested that He takes us one by one and arranges for every detail of our life. To Him, there are no little things. The God of the infinite is the God of the infinitesimal. He cannot forget the saints whom he has engraven on the palms of his hands.

> I know not where His islands lift
> Their fronded palms in the air,
> I only know, I cannot drift
> Beyond His love and care.

If the Lord careth for thee, be thyself at rest.

. . . There was silence and I heard a voice . . . (Job 4:16).

George Fox in the first pages of his journal says, "I walked abroad in solitary places many days and often took my Bible and sat in hollow trees and lonesome places till night came on." It was in one of these lonesome places that he made his great discovery, "There is one, even Christ Jesus, who can speak to thy condition."

Be still, relax and listen for His voice. Wait in expectant silence.

> God must have deeply loved the silences
> A stillness on the sunset and the dawn.
>
> God must have deeply loved the silences,
> For is there one of us who has not heard
> Promptings to silence that he speak not of?
>
> *Mavis C. Barnett.*

He who has graduated in the science of silence is himself a wise man.

I have become absolutely convinced that neither death nor life, neither messenger of heaven, nor monarch of earth, neither what happens today nor may happen tomorrow; neither a power from on high, nor a power from below, nor anything else in God's whole world has any power to separate us from the love of God in Christ Jesus our Lord (Rom. 8:38-39—Phillips' Trans.).

The celebrated Halyburton of Scotland welcomed scores of visitors to that room in St. Andrew's where they stood around his bedside and listened to words that seemed to be inspired by a glimpse of heaven from the land of Beulah. None of his previous sermons equalled his discoursings from that bed of suffering. "This is the best pulpit," said he, "that I was ever in. I am laid on this bed for this very end, that I may commend my Lord."

He called it a shaking hands with the King of Terrors. After a night of agonizing pain he said to his wife, "Jesus came to me in the third watch of the night, walking upon the waters; and He said to me, 'I am Alpha and Omega, the beginning and the end, and I have the keys of death.' He stilled the tempest in my soul, and there is a great calm. I have ripened fast under the bright sun of righteousness, and had brave showers."   *Dr. T. L. Cuyler.*

Make a pulpit of every circumstance.

Looking for that blessed hope and the glorious appearing of the great God and our Saviour Jesus Christ (Titus 2:13).

He is coming! He is on the road and traveling quickly. The sound of His approach should be as music to our hearts! Ring out, ye bells of hope.

> Faith looks back and says,
>   "Christ died for me."
> Above and cries,
>   "He lives for me";
> Forward and whispers,
>   "He comes for me."

We are not traveling by schedule but by faith.

He hath filled the hungry with good things, and the rich he hath sent empty away (Luke 1:53).

"Tell me," says Anthony, "how you live. How spend you your time?" "Verily sir," replied the little man, "I have no good works. I am a poor, humble, hard-working cobbler, with no ability to do any great thing. I just live from day to day as God helps me. I am up at the dawn. I pray for the city, my neighbors, my family, myself; I eat my scanty victuals, and then I sit me down to my hard labor all the day, and when the dusk shuts down, I eat again the bit I have earned and thank God and pray and sleep. I keep me ever, by God's help, from all false-honesty. And so I live, never fearing that it will not bring me out, at last, into the everlasting light."

Then turned away the long-bearded monk, "Ah, me! that one life of man should be so humbly full, and another so proudly empty!"

People who are right with themselves are usually right with the world. Being out of sorts with others is a symptom of being out of sorts with oneself.

Remember ye not the former things neither consider the things of old (Isa. 43:18).

O Thou Divine Companion, we praise thee for thy constant presence throughout life's journey.

Help us to . . . be freed from the things that cling to us like the hard dead shells of the barnacles and hold us back. Wilt thou remove them and make us seaworthy as we push on into open seas to new opportunities and greater responsibilities. *D. W. P.*

> My soul is sailing through the sea
> But the past is heavy and hindereth me.
> The past hath crusted cumbrous shells
> That hold the flesh of cold sea-mells
>   About my soul.
> The huge waves wash, the high waves roll,
> Each barnacle clingeth and worketh dole
>   And hindereth me from sailing!
>
> Old past let go and drop i' the sea
> Till fathomless waters cover thee!
> For I am living but thou art dead;
> Thou drawest back, I strive ahead
>   The day to find
> Thy shells unbind! Night comes behind,
> I needs must hurry with the wind
>   And trim me best for sailing.
>   *Sidney Lanier*

I have set my sails. All winds that blow shall drive me forward.

He . . . carried them all the days . . . (Isa. 63:9).

The picture of Jesus with the little ones in his arms is very beautiful. Jesus takes a child in His arms; there is love, tenderness, protection. The bosom is the place of warmth, of affection, of intimacy, of confidence. The encircling arms imply safety, support, shelter. He lifted up a child and held it in his arms; so he carries His people through this world. He does not merely tell them how to go, but He takes them on His shoulders, carrying not their burdens only, but themselves. Thus He bears them on through life and through death.   *J. R. Miller.*

> Carried by Jesus, all the days,
>   Yes, underneath are His loving arms!
> Carried so safe through the misty haze
>   Thine heart shall be free from all alarms.   *E. H. T.*

Instead of trying to escape from our problems, let us try encompassing them with God.

O how love I thy law! It is my meditation all the day (Psalm 119:97).

Wrote James Gilmour of Mongolia: "When I feel I cannot make headway in my devotion, I open at the Psalms and push in my canoe, and let myself be carried along in the stream of devotion which flows through the whole book. The current always sets toward God, and in most places is strong and deep.

> I opened the old, old Bible
>   And looked at a page of Psalms;
> Till the wintry sea of my trouble,
>   Was soothed as by summer calms,
>
> For the words that have helped so many,
>   And that ages have made more dear,
> Seemed new in their power to comfort,
>   And they brought me their word of cheer.
>
> *Marianne Farmingham.*

Affliction opens the Bible at the right places.

He loved his own that were in the world and loved them in the highest degree (John 13:1—Translation by St. John Chrysostom).

Our Father God looks after the little as well as the big. He makes the tides in the sea and shapes the wing of the sparrow. Nothing is big enough to defy him and nothing is so little as to escape Him. The ray of light from the farthest solar system and the blush on the primrose alike reveal his radiance. Back of it all is His infinite, everlasting personal love. Why should we ever forget Him, or think that anything is too difficult for Him, or fear that He has forgotten us?   *Joseph Anderson Vance.*

> There's not a bird, with lonely nest
> In pathless wood or mountain crest,
> Nor meaner thing, which does not share
> O God, in Thy paternal care.

Love holds the field when all else dies.

. . . I have redeemed thee, I have called thee by thy name; thou art mine (Isa. 43:1).

Lord I love thy morning
   When the sun breaks through;
When the birds are glad with singing,
   And the grass is wet with dew;
When the world is full of living,
   And all nature seems to pray,
"Thou hast kept us through the darkness,
   Father guide us through the day."
For it always will remind me
   It was morning in my soul,
On the day I met my Saviour,
   When He touched and made me whole.

Whenever you complete the job of cleaning your soulhouse, you may expect company.

. . . In whatsoever state I am, therein to be content (Phil. 4:11, RV—Be content in it even if not with it.)

S omewhere or other in the worst flood of trouble, there is always a dry spot for contentment to get its foot on; and if there were not, it would learn to swim. This is learning to be content, whatever the circumstances may be.

> Strong grows the oak in the sweeping storm,
> Safely the flower sleeps under the snow,
> And the farmer's hearth is never warm
> Till the cold wind starts to blow.   *Josiah Gilbert Holland.*

It has been said that no man is safe unless he can stand anything that can happen to him. The Christian is more than safe, for he can use anything that can happen to him. *Everything is grist to his mill.*

And my people shall dwell in a peaceable habitation, and in sure dwellings and in quiet resting places (Isa. 32:18).

> 'Mid all the traffic of the ways,
>   Turmoils without, within,
> Make in my heart a quiet place,
>   And come and dwell therein;
>
> A little shrine of quietness,
>   All sacred to Thyself,
> Where Thou shalt all my soul possess,
>   And I may find myself;
>
> A little shelter from life's stress,
>   Where I may lay me prone,
> And bare my soul in loneliness,
>   And know as I am known.
>
> A little place of mystic grace,
>   Of self and sin swept bare,
> Where I may look upon Thy face,
>   And talk with Thee in prayer.   *John Oxenham.*

That is not weakness which calls you into solitude to meditate and pray.

. . . The Lord hath His way in the whirlwind and in the storm, and the clouds are the dust of His feet (Nah. 1:3).

> When tempest's clouds are dark and high,
>   His bow of love and peace
> Shines sweetly in the vaulted sky;
>   A pledge that storms shall cease.

The promises are just the same 'pon the dull days as 'pon the fine shiny ones, every bit, and do hold just so good as ever. The bank o' Heaven isn't broke because the sun is clouded up a bit. Though we do get cast down, and though the devil do hale us off to the dungeon an' tell us that we shall never get out no more, bless 'ee, Frankey, he's a ould liar, and you can never believe a word he do say.   *D. Quorm.*

Pains and sorrow die of inattention; joys and gratitudes grow through attention.

Instead of the thorn . . . (Isa. 55:13).

> The withered flowers hold the seeds of promise,
>   The winter days are harbingers of spring;
> The trials that may often seem most bitter
>   May bring to you the joys that make you sing.
>
> The sorrows that have come to you unbidden
>   Have often brought a peace before unknown;
> The Maker of your destiny is striving
>   To fit your heart to be His royal throne.
>
> Your roses may have thorns, but don't forget—
>   Your thorns may have some roses, too;
> The Lord of great compassion loves you yet,
>   And He will never fail to see you through.

The best rosebush after all, is not that which has the fewest thorns, but that which bears the finest roses.

And he said unto them, Why are ye so fearful? how is it that ye have no faith? (Mark 4:40).

> Why do we worry about the nest?
>   We only stay for a day;
> Or a month, or a year, at the Lord's behest,
>   In this habitat of clay.
>
> Why do we worry about the road,
>   With its hills or deep ravine?
> In a dismal path, or heavy load,
>   We are helped by hands unseen.
>
> Why do we worry about the years
>   That our feet have not yet trod?
> Who labors with courage and trusts, not fears,
>   Has fellowship with God.

We will never know victory over anxiety until we begin to treat it as sin. For such it is. It is deep-seated distrust of the tender care of the Father who assures us again and again that even the falling sparrow is in His tender love and care.

The beginning of anxiety is the end of faith. The beginning of faith is the end of anxiety.

Thou leddest them . . . to give them light in the way wherein they should go (Neh. 9:12).

People have found, in real life, that God never lets a faithful disciple down—never! This faith guides through the blackest night.

A minister once went from a town into the backwoods to preach, and found it necessary to return at night when it was very dark. A backwoodsman provided him with a torch of pitch-pine wood. The minister, who had never seen anything like it exclaimed, "It will soon burn out!" "It will light you home," came the confident answer. "The wind may blow it out," said the preacher. "It will light you home," again came the answer. "But what if it should rain?" "It will light you home!" And it did. The man who had walked by that light knew that he could depend on it. *So can you count on the down-to-earth God to light your way through, and guide you home.*

And when the cloud was taken up from over the tabernacle, the children of Israel went onward in all their journeys (Exod. 40:36).

> The road that we have come is closed and guarded;
>   God closes it behind us as we go.
> The heart still clings closely to the things discarded,
>   But God says, "Onward, life must move and grow."
>
> We might turn back and tear away the fences,
>   Retrieve the things of dear, remembered days;
> But we would find dead husks to feed our senses
>   As the reward for all our rebel ways.
>
> The road leads on. That is the one direction
>   In which God keeps it open for our tread.
> Fatal is any turning or deflection.
>   Our shining destinies are all ahead.

Clarence Edwin Flynn.

The start is important, but it is the finish that counts.

For consider him that endured such contradiction of sinners against himself, lest ye be wearied and faint in your minds (Heb. 12:3).

There are times in one's life when all the world seems to turn against us. Our motives are misunderstood, our words misconstrued. A malicious smile or an unkind word reveals to us the unfriendly feelings of others. Our advances are repulsed or met with icy coldness; a dry refusal arrests on our lips the offer of help.

Courage, patience, poor disconsolate one! God is making a furrow in your heart, where He will surely sow His grace. It is rare when injustice, or slights patiently borne, do not leave the heart at the close of the day filled with marvelous joy and peace. It is the seed God has sown, springing up and bearing fruit.

A disappointment, a contradiction, a harsh word received and endured as in His presence, is worth more than a long prayer.

. . . Most gladly will I glory in my infirmities . . . (2 Cor. 12:9).

Make allowance for the infirmities of the flesh, which are purely physical. To be fatigued, body and soul, is not sin, to be in heaviness is not sin.

The Christian life is not a feeling, it is a principle; when your hearts will not fly, let them go and if they will neither fly nor go, be sorry for them and be patient with them, and take them to Christ as you would carry your little lame child to a tenderhearted, skillful surgeon. Does the surgeon, in such a case, upbraid the child for being lame?
Elizabeth Prentiss.

> Three men were walking on a wall,
> Feeling, Faith and Fact,
> When Feeling got an awful fall,
> And Faith was taken back.
> So close was Faith to Feeling,
> He stumbled and fell too,
> But Fact remained,
> And pulled Faith back
> And Faith brought Feeling too.

Be at leisure and know that I am God (Psalm 46:10—Kay's Trans.).

The late Dr. Jowett said that once he was in a most pitiful perplexity, and consulted Dr. Berry. "What would you do if your were in my place?" he entreated.

"I don't know, Jowett. I am not there, and you are not there yet. When do you have to act?"

"On Friday."

"Then you will find your way perfectly clear on Friday. The Lord will not fail you," answered Berry.

And sure enough, on Friday all was plain.

One of the greatest and wisest of all Queen Victoria's diplomatists has left it on record that it became an inveterate habit of his mind, never to allow any opinion on any subject to crystallize until it became necessary to arrive at a practical decision.

F. W. Boreham.

And as many as walk according to this rule, peace be on them . . . (Gal. 6:16).

The name of Dr. Frank Crane will long merit a household familiarity. He was a journalist by training, a student of human nature by inclination and a wizard in helpful philosophy. Out of his fertile mind came many golden rules of living, which will remain virile until the end of time.

Not long before his death, Dr. Crane wrote precepts for old age. "When I am old," says the resolution, "I will observe the following ideals (perhaps)":

1. I will not try to act nor dress nor talk so as to make people think I am younger than I am.

2. I will not pretend to be young, nor be angry when called old, nor ashamed of my age.

3. I will not complain of being old.

4. I will not continually remind people of my old age to secure their sympathy, or to hear them say I am not so old after all or do not seem so.

5. I will not form the habit of indulging in reminiscences.

6. I will be particularly careful not to repeat the same anecdote over and over.

7. I will not complain of the present and claim the past was much better.

8. If I am deaf, weak-eyed, lame, or otherwise afflicted, I will not advertise my infirmities, but avoid obtruding them upon the notice of others as much as possible.

9. I will not talk of myself, my work, my achievements, even of my mistakes, any more than necessary.

10. I will speak cheerfully or keep still.

11. I will never indulge in cynicism, never sneer at youth and will always try to appreciate what younger folks do.

12. I shall concede my life's triumph to be growing triumphantly, victoriously old.

13. In a word, I shall try to adjust myself to old age, as well as to all other facts of life.

. . . No plan of his can be hindered . . . (Job 42:2—RV).

I believe that Jesus who is Head over all things to His Church, has the program of my best possible future which involves these two elements—His highest glory, through me, and my highest happiness in Him. *Daniel Steele.*

God's plan for my life is undefeatable.

A soldier on service in the spiritual army is never off his battlefield.

Whom I shall see for myself . . . (Job 19:27).

> Tho' the road may be rough where He leads me,
>   Still His footprints I plainly can trace,
> And the trials I meet will seem nothing,
>   When I look in my dear Saviour's face.
>
> So I keep my eyes fixed upon Jesus,
>   While I'm running life's wearisome race;
> I'll forget the hard pathway I traveled,
>   When I look in my dear Saviour's face.
>
> Tho' the shadows around me may gather,
>   Safe I rest in my Lord's secret place,
> For I know there'll be glorious sunshine,
>   When I look in my dear Saviour's face.
>
> When I look in His face, His wonderful face,
>   In Heaven, that beautiful place!
> All the hardships of earth will seem nothing—
>   When I look in my dear Saviour's face.

The path of sorrow and that path alone leads to the land where sorrow is unknown.

How precious also are thy thoughts unto me, O God! how great is the sum of them! If I should count them they are more in number than the sand: when I awake I am still with thee (Psalm 139:17, 18).

A story from a children's book tells of a railway into Edinburgh, Scotland, which goes through a long tunnel before coming into the city. There was a certain old lady who lived in the country, who had a great dread of the long, dark tunnel. So, although her friends laughed at her, and tried to tease her out of it, she always used to get out at Abbeyhill, before the tunnel, and go into town by taxi.

One day when the train reached Abbeyhill, she was sleeping and her friends did not awaken her. So she passed through the tunnel she so much feared, in her sleep and never knew it, and when she opened her eyes, she was in the city.

Fear can hamstring the soul.

Let the beauty of the Lord our God be upon us . . . (Psalm 90:17).

One day a wanderer found a lump of clay so fragrant that its odors scented all the room. Then whence this wondrous perfume—say! Friend, if the secret I disclose, I have been dwelling with the rose. Sweet parable! And will not those who love to dwell with Sharon's rose distill sweet perfume all around, though low and mean themselves are found?

It was said of Chesterfield, the heartless dandy, upon his return from visiting Fenelon, the archbishop of Cambrai: "If I had stayed another day in his presence I am afraid I would have had to become a Christian, his spirit was so pure, so attractive and so beautiful."

. . . The prisoner of Jesus . . . (Eph. 3:1).

Why are there so many prisons in life? Why do we so often find ourselves in chains of sorrow, suffering,, hardship and difficulty?

God has many lessons to teach us in the prison, which we could not learn outside. If you take these times of bondage and darkness in the right light, you will soon find the lessons for yourself, and then the prison-life will have accomplished God's purposes.

Many people fret and mourn when they find their freedom cut off and the gloomy prison walls shutting them in. They miss God's meaning; they do not learn His lessons. Often then, the time of captivity has to be prolonged.

However dense the darkness is, it cannot shut out God. We may be cut off from every human friend, but not from Him. His people are never put out of reach of Himself.

Do not be afraid of His prisons. Get into His purpose for you and you will grow stronger, more patient there.

By Him therefore, let us offer the sacrifice of praise to God continually, that is, the fruit of our lips, giving thanks to His name (Heb. 13:15).

Sing through the darkness and sing in the light—
Sing with the morning and sing in the night;
Sing when your eyes have been clouded with pain,
Sing in the sunshine and sing through the rain;
Sing when it's autumn, or winter, or spring—
Nothing can touch you so long as you sing!

What though the roads may be dark when you travel,
What though your hopes may grow snarled and unravel?
What though the hills you must climb will be steep,
What though life promises you little but sleep?
Sing to the future, and what it may bring—
Nothing can break you, so long as you sing!

Margaret E. Sangster.

When Robert Ingersoll died, the printed notice of the funeral read, "There will be no singing."

A sad world cannot be sweetened by a sour religion.

. . . Take root downward and bear fruit upward (Isa. 37:31).

W hy is it that the mountain hemlocks can attain such stateliness in spite of fierce winter gales and crushing snows? If you look at one of them closely you will see that it has foliage almost as delicate as a fir, its dark needles being as dainty as fairy feathers. Yet, if you try to break a twig or a bough you will learn that therein lies the strength and the tenacious power of the hemlock. It will bend and yield, but it will not break. Winds may whip and toss it this way and that, but they cannot break it—nor can elements, however fierce, pull its roots out of the ground. Secure and undaunted it stands. For months it may have its graceful form held down by a mighty weight of snow, but when the warm breath of summer winds, and the melting influence of summer's sun, relieve it of its burden, it straightens up, as proud and as noble as it was before.

Beautiful, wonderful hemlock of the mountains—what a lesson you bring to us! *Though we may be storm-tossed and bent by the winds of adversity, we need not be crushed and broken, if our souls are anchored to the Rock of Ages.*

For our . . . affliction which is but for a moment, worketh for us a far more exceeding and eternal weight of glory (2 Cor. 4:17).

A crippled boy sat in his wheelchair on the ferryboat and a sympathetic lady pitying his helplessness, exclaimed to her friend, "Poor fellow! What has he to look forward to?" The cripple overheard it and turning his head, said pleasantly, "Wings, some day."

Pray not for crutches, but for wings!

> Our burdens are our blessings in disguise;
> Through battle, smoke, and fire we win the heavenly prize.
> The weights of glory come from weights of woe;
> Our Edens, from transfigured thorns below.
> O suffering saint, take up the trying things
> Until they grow from weights to heavenly wings.

God give me serenity to accept the things I cannot change, courage to change those I can, and wisdom to know the difference.

_____

To everything there is a season, and a time to every purpose, under the heaven (Eccl. 3:1).

In winter there are no roses blooming in the deserted, wind-swept, snow-covered garden. Nor in summer do crystal snowflakes fly. Each season has its own work, its own beauty, and by hands of another season this work cannot be done, this beauty cannot be breathed.

And so of man's life. Each season has its own duties and its own joys, and if they are not laid hold of, no other season can make up the loss; they are gone down the dim, untraveled river of Forever.

Each day, indeed, has its own duty, its own smile, its own tear, its own heart throb. If only it be lived in for itself, life would be fuller and richer in everything; and the clusters of blessedness hanging from the boughs of each day would proclaim life's every season to have wrought well, and to deserve well, for what lies before.

Alas! that we let the burdening tomorrows crush the energy and strength out of today, so that its work is undone or marringly done. *Give your today a chance.* Give it only its own work to do, and evening will find you laughing over the beauty and faithfulness that smiles up to you from the well-done duties; and the eternal tomorrow will meet you with the kisses of tenderness, not with wounding blows.

. . . The gate shall not be shut until the evening (Ezek. 46:2).

Do you say that the best is behind us?
Is it true that life's beauty is gone?
Is it sad that the morning is over—
That the twilight is gathering on?

When you turn from the flowers and sunshine,
And you walk with your face to the shade,
And you think of the gladness departed—
Is it true that your heart is afraid?

O I say that the best is before us!
We have not yet dreamed of the best—
Of the beautiful days that are coming,
Though our pathway winds down to the West.

It is farther away than the sunset;
It is past all the hush of the night;
When the sleep and the silence are over,
We shall open our eyes to the light.   *Edith Hickman Divall.*

Let us walk into our sunset with our shoulders back and our heads up!

Wait on the Lord: be of good courage, and he shall strengthen thine heart: wait, I say, on the Lord (Psalm 27:14).

One day an energetic man suffered an acute heart attack. For days his life hung in the balance. Even after the greatest danger had passed, he was forced to be completely quiet. Later on he said to me, "I could not lift my hand; but God chose to lift my mind and heart. At first I could do nothing but lie in the darkness of my own spirit and wonder. Out of the darkness, God spoke to me. In the stillness I was able for the first time in my life, to see things for their true worth.

"Up to that time, I had been busy with the noise of mere doing and going. But God had been waiting all along to help me—but I was too busy to hear.

"Those weeks of enforced quiet saved my life. What is more important, they saved it for its true usefulness. Out of physical defeat came spiritual victory."

God only can bring spiritual victory out of physical defeat.

. . . Let me die the death of the righteous and let my last end be like his (Num. 23:10).

Daniel Webster's last few days were spent in a fight by his powerful constitution against the inevitable. The last time he walked feebly from his bed to his window, he called out to his man servant: "I want you to moor my yacht down there where I can see it from my window; then I want you to hoist the flag at the masthead, and every night to hang the lamp up in the rigging; when I go down I want to go down with my colors flying and my lamp burning."

He told them to put on his monument, "Lord I believe; help thou my unbelief."

In the final moment he started up from his pillow long enough to say: "I still live." He does live and will ever live in the grateful memories of his countrymen.

We are immortal until our work is done, but since we have eternal work to do, we are eternally immortal.

. . . I have laid help upon one that is mighty . . . (Psalm 89:19).

G od of our life there are days when the burdens we carry chafe our shoulders and weigh us down, when the road seems dreary and endless, the skies gray and threatening; when our lives have no music in them and our hearts are lonely and our souls have lost their courage.

Flood the path with light, we beseech thee; turn our eyes to where the skies are full of promise; tune our hearts to brave music; give us the sense of companionship with heroes and saints and the common people of every age; and so quicken us that we may be able to encourage the souls of all who journey with us, on the road of life.

Knit up for us our raveled sleeve of care with the calm of eternity.

The glad heart maketh a cheerful countenance . . . (Prov. 15:13).

If I knew that a word of mine
A word not kind and true,
Might leave its trace
On a loved one's face,
I'd never speak harshly,
    Would you?

If I knew the light of a smile
Might linger the whole day through,
And lighten some heart
With a heavier part
I wouldn't withhold it,
    Would you?

The best kind of smiles are not "put on." They come out because they are "in." They are the result of a satisfied, thankful and glad heart. They are the exterior expression of an interior joy, which glows and grows as the days go by. When we are contented at the center, the countenance will be calmly cheerful. This interior gladness comes only in one way—through being right with God and man. *"Oh look unto Him and ye shall beam with joy"* is Cheyne's translation of Psalm 34:5.   *B. M'Call Barbour.*

Do not fret therefore in view of tomorrow for tomorrow will have its own anxieties. The day's peculiar troubles suffice for that day (Matt. 6:34— Berkeley version).

I found myself the other evening staggering alone under a load that was heavy enough to crush half a dozen strong men. Out of sheer exhaustion, I put it down and had a good look at it. I found that it was all borrowed!

Part of it belonged to the following day; part of it belonged to the following week; and here was I borrowing it that it might crush me now! It is a very stupid but a very ancient (and also modern!) blunder.   *F. W. Boreham.*

The winds of disquietude are laid to sleep in the caverns of Divine Faithfulness.

. . . They took knowledge of them that they had been with Jesus (Acts 4:13).

S ome years ago, at a social function, one of England's leading actors was asked to recite for the pleasure of his fellow guests. He consented and asked if there was anything special that his audience would like to hear. After a moment's pause, an aged minister arose and said, "Could you, sir, recite the Twenty-Third Psalm?"

A strange look passed over the great actor's face. He paused for a moment, and then said, "I can, and I will upon one condition— after I have recited it, you, my friend, will do the same."

Impressively, the great actor began the Psalm. His voice and his intonation were perfect. He held his audience spellbound, and as he finished, a great burst of applause broke from the guests.

Then, as it died away, the aged minister arose and began to recite. His voice was not remarkable; his intonation was not faultless. When he finished, no sound of applause broke the silence, but there was not a dry eye in the room, and many heads and hearts were bowed in reverential awe!

The great actor rose to his feet. His voice shook with uncontrollable emotion as he laid his hand upon the shoulder of the aged minister, and said to the audience, "I have reached your eyes and ears, my friends. This man has reached your hearts. The difference is just this: *"I know the twenty-third Psalm, but he knows the Shepherd."*

He took the blind man by the hand and led him out of the town . . . (Mark 8:23).

T hat was a very gentle thing to do. Look closely at the picture—Jesus leading a poor blind man along the street. What thoughts does it start in our minds? The blind man represents each one of us in our sinful state—in the midst of a world of beauty, but seeing nothing; groping in the gloom, unable to find the way alone; doomed to perish in the darkness, unless someone takes us by the hand and leads us. As Jesus came to this man in his blindness, so He comes to each one of us, offering to take us by the hand and be our guide, to lead us, through the gloom and the dangers, home to light and glory. We can never stumble in the darkness if He leads us. *J. R. Miller.*

> Whate'er my God ordains is right;
>   His Will is ever just
> Howe'er He orders now my cause,
>   I will be still and trust.
>   He is my God;
>   Though dark my road,
> He holds me that I shall not fall;
> Wherefore to Him I leave it all. *S. Rodigast.*

Affliction recruits hope.

. . . Thy faithfulness reacheth unto the clouds (Psalm 36:5).

The Psalmist gave the great assurance, "He that dwelleth in the secret place of the most High shall abide under the shadow of the Almighty." That Scripture inspired Sidney Lanier to say, "I will build me a nest on the greatness of God." We ought not to worry. God will take care of us. It is important only that we are His and obey and do our best. His way may be "mysterious," but be sure that with infinite wisdom and infinite goodness He plans for His own.

A dauntless faith in God brushes fear aside like the cobwebs in a giant's path.

So whether on the hilltops high and fair
I dwell, or in the sunless valleys where
The shadows lie, what matter? He is there.

Search me, O God, and know my heart: try me and know my thoughts: And see if there be any wicked way in me and lead me in the way everlasting (Psalm 139:23, 24).

Anything cherished in the heart which is contrary to the will of God, let it seem ever so insignificant, or be ever so deeply hidden, will cause us to fall before our enemies. Any conscious root of bitterness, cherished toward another, any self seeking, any harsh judgments, any slackness in obeying the voice of the Lord, any doubtful habits or surroundings—these things will effectually cripple and paralyze our spiritual life.

We may have hidden the evil in the most remote corner of our hearts and may have covered it over from our sight, refusing even to recognize its existence, although we cannot help being all the time secretly aware that it is there. We may steadily ignore it, and persist in declarations of consecration and full trust; we may be more earnest than ever in our religious duties, and have the eyes of our understanding opened more and more to the truth and the beauty of life and walk of faith. We may seem to have reached an almost impregnable position of victory and yet we may find ourselves suffering bitter defeats. Nothing will do any good until the wrong thing is dug up from its hiding place, brought out to light and laid before God. *Hannah Whitehall Smith.*

God spares our weakness by only showing us our own deformity by degrees and as He gives strength to bear the sight. He only shows us to ourselves, so to say, by bits; here one and there another as He undertakes our correction.

_____

. . . I believe God . . . (Acts 27:25).

O n one of those awful sleepless nights, tossed as the ship was like a cockle-shell on the raging sea, the angel of God stood by Paul with words of cheer and courage: "Fear not, Paul." Though Paul suffered, he was never forsaken. He was promised all who sailed with him. When he announced the good news to the trembling and terror-stricken passengers, his simple words were, "I believe God"—the language of pure, unaffected faith.

From that point on Paul seems to have taken charge of affairs and no doubt by his sound judgment and wise advice, he was the means of saving the lives of all.

What a blessing is one strong man of faith! When in such a storm, "all hope that we should be saved was . . . taken away" his "I believe God," is an example of how faith works.

Faith has nothing to do with circumstances; it deals entirely with the Word of God.

. . . Thou hast the dew of thy youth (Psalm 110:3).

To be seventy years young is sometimes far more cheerful and hopeful than to be forty years old.   *Oliver Wendell Holmes.*

Old—are we growing old?
Life blooms as we travel on
Up the hills, into fresh, lovely dawn;
We are children who do but begin
The sweetness of life to win.
Because heaven is in us, to bud and unfold,
We are younger for growing old!

We have a God who lives in Eternity and knows no age-limit.

Have no anxiety about anything, but in everything by prayer and supplication with thanksgiving let your requests be made known unto God. . . . And my God shall supply every need of yours according to His riches in glory in Christ Jesus (Phil. 4:6, 19—RSV).

The Lord in that great Sermon on the Mount said, "Be not therefore anxious for the morrow, for the morrow will be anxious for itself. Sufficient unto the day is the evil thereof."

While we worry, we do not trust. Still, we are inclined to worry—we who have burdens and responsibilities.

Bishop Quayle had a sense of humor concerning himself. So he tells humorously of a time when he sat in his study worrying over many things. He says that finally the Lord came to him and said, *"Quayle, you go to bed; I'll sit up the rest of the night."*

The Lord is in His holy temple, let all the earth keep silence before Him (Hab. 2:20).

There is a God, all nature cries,
I see it painted on the skies,
I see it in the flowering spring,
I hear it when the birdlings sing,
I see it in the flowing main,
I see it on the fruitful plain,
I see it stamped on hail and snow,
I see it where the streamlets flow,
I see it in the clouds that soar,
I hear it when the thunders roar,
I see it when the morning shines,
I see it when the day declines,
I see it in the mountain's height,
I see it in the smallest mite,
I see it everywhere abroad,
I feel—I know, there is a God.

The believer does not believe because he feels, he feels because he believes.

For in Him we live and move and have our being . . . (Acts 17:28).

S ocrates at an extreme age, learned to play a musical instrument; Cato, at eighty years of age, thought it proper to learn the Greek language; Plutarch when between the ages of seventy and eighty, commenced the study of Latin; Sir Henry Spelman neglected the sciences in his youth, but commenced the study of them when he was between fifty and sixty and became a most learned scholar. Gladstone took up the study of a new language at seventy. Titian, the artist, lived to be ninety-nine, painting right up to the end. Franklin did not commence his philosophical pursuits until he had reached his fiftieth year. Dryden wrote his most pleasing productions in his old age. Unlike the flesh, the spirit does not decay with years. We can keep on living abundantly and creatively, until we die, no matter at what age!

> What then, shall we sit idly down and say,
> The night hath come; it is no longer day?
> For age is opportunity no less
> Than youth itself, though in another dress.
> And as the evening twilight fades away,
> The sky is filled with stars invisible by day.

Our life can be full and fresh and dew-touched until its close.

Therefore it is of faith . . . to the end the promise might be sure . . . (Rom. 4:16).

When the great chemist, Sir Michael Faraday was on his deathbed, some journalists questioned him as to his speculations concerning the soul and death. "Speculations!" said the dying man in astonishment, "I know nothing about speculations; I am resting on certainties."

> I want the proved certainties
>   To soothe the soul's deep cries;
> And not man's vain philosophies
>   Based only on surmise.
>
> I want a book that is inspired
>   In which to posit faith;
> And not some mutilated scroll,
>   Or literary wraith.
>
> I want the calm assurance of
>   A voice beyond this dust,
> A voice from out eternity
>   In which to place my trust.
>
> For when I come, at eventide
>   To Jordan's swollen stream,
> I want the tested verities,
>   And not some mystic dream.
>
> This mortal life is far too brief,
>   Eternity too vast,
> To follow human sophistries
>   And lose the soul at last.
>
> Then give me back the Holy Book
>   By inspiration penned;
> I'm through with fabled falsities,
>   And allegoric trend.   *M. D. Clayburn.*

If an angel should fly from heaven and inform the saint personally of the Savior's love, the evidence would not be one whit more satisfactory than that which is borne in the heart by the Holy Ghost.   *Spurgeon.*

He went about making things beautiful (Acts 10:38—RV).

G od is the God of beauty. His finger-prints of beauty are on all
the face of nature. Jesus, walking in the footsteps of God His
Father, went about making things exquisitely and immortally
beautiful.

He did not go about making beautiful things. No, He took things
existing and fashioned them into enduring beauty. He never
quarreled with God as to this world, for it furnished Him with a
platform on which to display his beauty-making power. He took
things as they were and made them the things they ought to be. In
a world of finished beauty, there would be no room for creative
beauty. He re-made the world He found, contented to work on
what was at hand. He asked for nothing more than to transform
what He found into divine beauty.

He was willing to live in a little provincial, despised, uncouth,
village of three thousand people, which bore the scorn of men, as
they sneeringly asked, "Can any good thing come out of
Nazareth?" But from this despised town of Palestine, He walked
forth and with this motto for His life word and work, "He went
about doing good." He made that town the city of all time.

*He found ugliness—He left beauty; He found pain—He left
pleasure; He found dirt—He left deity.*

. . . He is thy life and the length of thy days . . . (Deut. 30:20).

I have found beauty
In old trees that stand
Despite the ravages of winter's ice
And summer's devasting storms.
I have learned wisdom from trees
That draw their strength
From some sufficient source within;
Trees that spread their branches wide
Above a traveled lane,
Sharing with you and me the benedictions
Of sunshine and the rain. *Oma Carlyle Anderson.*

The wildest tempests, instead of tearing us from our foundations, only plant us deeper and root us more securely to the Rock of Ages.

It shall turn to you for a testimony (Luke 21:13).

The fiftieth milestone in my calendar of years had been reached when a message came to me from my Heavenly Father. For twenty-five years I had labored in fields afar with the gleaners in the whitened harvest fields, but now a Providence had changed the entire course of my life. I was confronted with the question, "After fifty years, what?"

I then read the following statement: "The greatest years of a woman's life come after fifty. Until that time she is accumulating new experiences. At fifty she has traveled every road. Now should come the harvest years. If a woman will keep intellectually alive, spiritually aglow and with heart aflame, with a passion for living service, she will see her greatest years from fifty to seventy-five."

Today in my eighty-second year I would bear witness to the fact that the years since that memorable experience—the crisis year— have been the richest, and the fullest and the sweetest of any of my long lifetime.

May this personal testimony be a star of hope to my fellow travelers toward sunrise.

Had I a thousand lives to give, Lord, they should all be Thine!
L. B. C.

Thine ears shall hear a word behind thee, saying, This is the way, walk ye in it, when ye turn to the right hand, and when ye turn to the left (Isa. 30:21).

I seem to have come to the cross-roads,
  And know not which way to turn,
So look into my Father's face,
  My direction from Him to learn.

I seem to have come to the cross-roads,
  And overhead clouds dark as night,
Then quickly I call to my Father
  To ask Him to send the light.

I seem to have come to the cross-roads,
  But the voice that I hear comforts me;
"Fear not! Be not afraid! I am with Thee
  As thy day, so shall thy strength be!"

I seem to have come to the cross-roads,
  But with words such as these, need I more,
For grace and courage to follow
  My Guide, Whose knowledge is sure!"
           E. Randall.

Are you in difficulty about your way? Go to God. He has promised, "I will instruct thee and teach thee in the way which thou shalt go: I will guide thee with mine eye."

And so the wise old road has taught me that whenever I come to the cross-roads, I shall find a sign post there.

_____

And the Lord shall guide thee continually and satisfy thy soul in drought, and make fat thy bones, and thou shalt be like a watered garden, and like a spring of water, whose waters fail not (Isa. 58:11).

Must all come to their close with lowered ideals and burnt-out hearts? In the companionship of God there is a continuous renewal for us in the spirit of the mind.

"He restoreth my soul." He carries on a process of recreation that defies the ravages of time. As the days go by, new flowers spring up within the soul and new song-birds build their nests among its boughs.

Jesus said, "Whosoever drinketh of the water that I shall give him shall never thirst." The picture of an inextinguishable vitality reappears with heightened color upon the glowing canvas of the Revelation. There "in the midst of the street" was the tree of life— there, where the crowds jostle, where traffic goes, where the multitude passes on heedless, hurrying feet. It is the last place one would think that verdure could appear. *It is the final word of inspiration concerning the invincible virility of the God-nourished soul.* *Dr. W. B. Hinson.*

When I remember thee upon my bed and meditate upon thee in the night watches (Psalm 63:6).

> Sleep cometh not when most I seem to need
>   Its kindly balm. Oh Father be to me
> Better than sleep and let these sleepless hours
>   Be hours of blessed fellowship with thee.

Thou hast been better than a dreamless night to my soul.
   Where the scars of the day are, let Thy healing love be laid.
Walk among our dreams O Christ, and keep them fair. *Let no dark shadow stain our lives in sleep or waking.*

Hitherto have ye asked nothing in my name; ask and ye shall receive that your joy may be full (John 16:24).

Alexander the Great had a famous, but indigent philosopher in his court. This adept in science was once particularly straightened in his circumstances. To whom alone should he apply but to his patron, the conqueror of the world? His request was no sooner made than granted. Alexander gave him a commission to receive of his treasury whatever he wanted. He immediately demanded in his sovereign's name ten thousand pounds. The treasurer, surprised at so large a demand, refused to comply, but waited upon the king and told him how unreasonable he thought the petition and how exorbitant the sum. Alexander listened with patience, but as soon as he heard the remonstrance replied, "Let the money be instantly paid. I am delighted with this philosopher's way of thinking; he has done me a singular honor; by the largeness of his request he shows the high idea he has conceived both of my superior wealth and my royal munificence."

Thus let us honor what the inspired calls the marvelous lovingkindness of God: "He that spared not his own Son, but delivered Him up for us all, how shall He not with Him freely give us all things?"

. . . Take no thought . . . for your Heavenly Father knoweth . . . (Matt. 6:31, 32).

Bishop Simpson wrote thus to his wife: "Be careful of your health; be cheerful; look up. The stars display their beauty to us only when we look at them; and if we look down at the earth, our hearts are never charmed.

Be resolved to be happy today, to be joyful now, and out of every fleeting moment draw all possible pure and lasting pleasure."

> I'll not confer with sorrow
>   Till tomorrow
> But joy shall have her way
>   This very day.

Our attitudes determine our altitudes.

For so an entrance shall be ministered unto you abundantly into the everlasting kingdom of our Lord and Saviour Jesus Christ (2 Peter 1:11).

L ife should begin in a very significant sense at seventy because the scholar should be graduating from the school of life with mind matured and heart enriched—in order to exercise a ministry impossible in the earlier years of scholastic endeavor. Nearly half a century of Christian life and labor should have removed the angularities and mellowed the mind of the scholar in that school in which the law is our teacher to bring us to Christ.

The dreams of youth unrealized so far, may find their fulfilment because of the daring confidence born of past years of experience of an Omnipotent, Omnipresent and Omniscient God.

At seventy we stand on the crest of the hill and thank God for the climb, the experiences, the developed powers, but we also look at the glorious view stretched out ahead, and expanded horizon, a beauty not even anticipated before, and greater heights and glories made possible and realizable, because of the glory of the grind behind.

If it is true that life may not last much longer at seventy, it is at least equally true that it ought to be deeper, higher and broader than at seventeen, or even at sixty-seven!

In the light of history in general and my own experience in particular, at seventy, I am faced by and accept a greater responsibility than ever before.   *Col. F. J. Miles.*

. . . My strength is made perfect in weakness . . . (2 Cor. 12:9).

I t appears almost certain that the weakness here recorded was bodily weakness, but Paul did not accept infirmity as an excuse for uselessness.

A naturalist asks, "How is it that the golden-crested wren, apparently so weak and helpless, can fly right across the North sea from Norway?" Because God knows how to fix strange energy within delicate organisms. Our very infirmities through our resolution and God's grace may give us special effectiveness.

> Give me a task too big
> Too hard for human hands.
> Then shall I come at length
> To lean on Thee;
> And leaning find my strength.   *W. H. Fowler.*

O taste and see that the Lord is good; blessed is the man that trusteth in Him (Psalm 34:8).

Often you cannot get at a difficulty so as to deal with it aright and find your way to a happy result. You pray, but have not the liberty in prayer which you desire. A definite promise is what you want. You try one and another of the inspired words, but they do not fit. You try again, and in due season a promise presents itself which seems to have been made for the occasion; it fits exactly as a well-made key fits the lock for which it was prepared. Having found the identical word of the living God, you hasten to plead it at the throne of grace, saying, "Oh, Lord, Thou hast promised this good thing unto Thy servant; be pleased to grant it!" The matter is ended; sorrow is turned to joy; prayer is heard.

C. H. Spurgeon.

Faith, mighty faith, the promise sees
   And looks to God alone,
Laughs at impossibilities,
   And cries, "It shall be done."

Try all you keys! Never despair! God leaves no treasurehouse locked against us.

. . . Stormy wind fulfilling His Word (Psalm 148:8).

I once lived in an old house in the country where the wind would sometimes whistle around. Thinking I would have some music if it must blow like that, I made a rude Aeolian harp of sewing silk strung across a board. I placed it under the slightly lifted sash of a north window and the music could be heard through all the house when the wild storms came!

Is there any north window in you life? Could you not so arrange the three wires of faith, hope and love that the storms of life should bring more music into this sad world? Many are doing it and perhaps more music than we dream of comes this way.

God has many an Aeolian harp. Will you be one?   *Crumbs.*

Of whom the world was not worthy . . . (Heb. 11:38).

"Eighty and six years have I served Christ," exclaimed the triumphant Polycarp; and he mounted the heavens in wreathing smoke and leaping flame rather than change his mind after so long and lovely an experience.

I saw the martyr at the stake.
The flames could not his courage shake,
Nor death his soul appall;
I asked him whence his strength was given,
He looked triumphantly to heaven,
And answered, "Christ is all."

Give me the spirit of those who were faithful unto death!

They climbed the steep ascent of heaven
Through peril, toil and pain.
Of God to us may grace be given
To follow in their train.

When you are in the furnace, remember God knows how much heat to turn on.

Why art thou cast down, O my soul and why art thou disquieted within me? Hope thou in God, for I shall yet praise him for the help of his countenance (Psalm 42:5).

After forty years of brilliant success the great composer Handel was down and out. His health was broken. His main financial supporter, Queen Caroline, was dead. He was deep in debt, and hungry. He felt a hundred years old, and hopelessly tired. There was no fire of inspiration left.

As he walked by a London church one day he groaned, "My God, My God, why hast thou forsaken me?" Hopelessly he returned to his shabby lodgings. There, on his desk, he found a bulky package. He broke the seal, drew out the contents. Here were the words for "A Sacred Oratorio." The author was asking Handel to write the music for it. Handel was indignant. He was not a religious man and just now was in no mood for religious meditation. Why had not the author written an opera instead?

But, as he began to turn the pages, a passage caught his eye, "He was despised and rejected of men . . . He looked for someone to have pity . . . He trusted in God . . . God did not leave his soul in Hell . . . He will give you rest . . . Wonderful, Counselor . . . I know that my Redeemer liveth . . . Rejoice . . . Hallelujah!"

Handel could feel the old fire rekindling. In his mind wondrous melodies tumbled over one another. Seizing a pen he started writing with amazing swiftness, page after page. For twenty-four days he labored, night and day, pausing only occasionally for a rest or a bite of food. At the end of the twenty-fourth day he threw himself on his bed exhausted. On his desk lay the score of the greatest oratorio ever written—"The Messiah." His last years were beset with many difficulties, but he never again gave in to despair. His resurrected faith remained victorious to the last.

God touched the broken spirit of an old man and filled it will quickening life. You may be old, or young—at any age. If you will let God touch your wintry despair with His love, you can have spring. *No matter how rough the world seems, or how many times it has beaten you, "this is the victory that overcometh the world, even our faith!"*

Whom the heaven must receive until the times of restitution of all things, which God hath spoken by the mouth of all his holy prophets since the world began (Acts 3:21).

> There's a light upon the mountains, and the day is at the
>   spring,
> When our eyes shall see the beauty and the glory of the
>   King,
> Weary was our heart with waiting, and the night-watch
>   seemed so long;
> But His triumph-day is breaking, and we hail it with a
>   song.
>
> There's a hush of expectation, and a quiet in the air.
> And the breath of God is moving, in the fervent breath of
>   prayer;
> For the suffering, dying Jesus, is the Christ upon the
>   throne,
> And the travail of our spirit is the travail of his own.
>
> Hark, we hear a distant music, and it comes with fuller
>   swell,
> 'Tis the triumph song of Jesus, of our King Immanuel!
> Zion, go ye forth to meet Him; and my soul, be swift to
>   bring,
> All thy sweetest and thy dearest for the triumph of our
>   King.   *Henry Burton.*

He shall come whose right it is to reign.

He . . . sat down under a juniper tree . . . (1 Kings 19:4).

This is Elijah! One is startled, perplexed, disappointed. Awhile ago we saw him on Mount Carmel surrounded by the thronging thousands of Israel, undismayed by the bold audacity of the worshippers of Baal, and confidently appealing to God to vindicate His own honor and confound Baalim. Here he is the prey of deep depression; forgetful of the past, giving all up, wanting God to take away his life. God has not once failed him. Not to any extent at all has one single foe prevailed against him.

Ought the child of God ever to feel depressed? If I am depressed, can I be trusting? Is not trust preventive of depression, as well as its antidote? We mark Elijah's great mistake. He should not have lost heart, should not have fled, should not have asked God to take away his life; all this was wrong. He should have remembered how God had wonderfully stood by him in the past and have firmly trusted Him still!

Is not his privilege ours also? May not God's people trust Him fully, firmly, under all circumstances and at all times? God is not afar off; neither has He forgotten to be gracious; and that which He has promised He will unfailingly remember and do. Are we not always in His hands and under His care? Should we ever have a single fear? Why should we be cast down or disquieted?   *J.T.W.*

Roll thy way upon Him, lean also upon Him and He gets it going (Psalm 37:5—Arabic).

A nother translation of this text reads, "Hand over everything to Him, in deep quiet trust."

> O there are heavenly heights to reach
>   In many a fearful place,
> While the poor, timid heir of God
>   Lies blindly on his face.
> Lies languishing for light Divine
>   That he shall never see
> Till he goes forward at Thy sign
>   And trusts himself to Thee.   *Rev. C. A. Fox.*

Faith is the courage of the spirit which projects itself forward, sure of finding the truth.   *Thomas Aquinas.*

To go bravely forward is to invite a miracle.

So teach us to number our days that we may apply our hearts unto wisdom (Psalm 90:12).

Today is a slender bridge which will bear its own load, but it will collapse if we add tomorrow's. In every year there are 365 letters from the King, each with its own message—"Bear this for me." What shall we do with the letters? Open them a day at a time. Yesterday's seal is broken; lay that letter reverently away; yesterday's cross is laid down, never to be borne again. Tomorrow's letter lies on the table; do not break the seal. For when tomorrow becomes today, there will stand beside us an unseen figure; and His hand will be on our brow, and His gaze will be in our eyes as He says with a loving smile, "As thy days, so shall thy strength be." The golden summary of our life is to be this: as to the past, a record of gratitude; as to the present, a record of service; and as to the future, a record of trust.   *D. M. Panton.*

Peace I leave with you, my peace I give unto you . . . (John 14:27).

Two artists agreed to paint pictures which would portray their respective conceptions of peace. The first painted a calm little pond, surrounded by woods and open plain. There was no sign of life in the picture, not even the indication that a breath of air was stirring. That was his idea of peace.

The other artist painted the scene of a windswept landscape, with a raging torrent in the foreground. A tree hung over the river bank and on a slender bough, just above its leaping rapids, sat two birds—singing! This latter picture represents true peace; the other depicts not peace but stagnation. In the midst of life's stormy sea we may know perfect peace always if Christ, who commanded the turbulent winds and the angry water to be muzzled, is our Pilot.

> At the heart of the cyclone tearing the sky,
> And flinging the clouds and towers by,
> Is a place of central calm.
> So here in the roar of mortal things,
> I have a place where my spirit sings—
> In the hollow of God's palm.

Thy peace can tread where there is no pathway.

Commit your way unto Him, relax also in Him, and he shall bring it (just as much as we commit) to pass (Psalm 37:5—as explained by David Cowie, D.D.).

The circumstances of her life she could not alter, but she took them to the Lord, and handed them over into His management; and then she believed that He took it, and she left all the responsibility, the worry and the anxiety with Him. As often as the anxieties returned, she took them back; and the result was that although the circumstances remained unchanged, her soul was kept in perfect peace in the midst of them.   *H.W.S.*

The hallmark of the follower of the Lord is his refusal to be weakened, or hardened, or soured, or made hopeless by disappointment.

. . . From Me is thy fruit found (Hosea 14:8).

Lord keep me sweet when I grow old,
   And things in life seem hard to bear;
When I feel sad and all alone,
   And people do not seem to care.

O keep me sweet when time has caused
   This body, which was once so strong,
To droop beneath its load of years,
   And suffering and pain have come.

And keep me sweet when I have grown
   To worry so, at din and noise;
And help me smile, the while I watch
   The noisy play of girls and boys.

Help me remember how that I,
   When I was younger than today,
And full of life and health and joy,
   Would romp and shout in happy play.

Help me to train my heart each day,
   That it will only sweetness hold;
And as the days and years roll on,
   May I keep sweet, as I grow old.

O keep me sweet, and let me look
   Beyond the frets that life must hold,
To see the glad eternal joys.
   Yes, keep me sweet in growing old.

Our faith is to make us easy to live with.

_____

. . . He stayeth his rough wind in the day of the east wind (Isa. 27:8).

I simply don't know what to do with myself when the wind is from the east," complained a nervous invalid. "Well, you can't stop the wind," replied the practical physician, "but you surely can get into a cozy south room as far away from it as possible, and find some pleasant employment."

This simple bit of advice is as good for the soul as for the body. There are east winds of gloom and unrest that will not down at command, but we can learn to retreat into some south corner of sunny memories or cheerful occupation until they pass.

J. R. Miller.

I must not be environmentally-conditioned, but God-conditioned.

For all the promises of God in Him are yea, and in Him, Amen . . . (2 Cor. 1:20).

S ometimes Christians go for a good while in trouble, yet not realizing that riches are laid up for them in a familiar promise.

When Christian and Hopeful strayed out of the path upon forbidden ground, they found themselves locked up in Doubting Castle by Giant Despair for their carelessness, and there they lay for days, until one night they began to pray. "Now a little before it was day, Good Christian as one half amazed, broke out in passionate speech: 'What a fool!' quoth he, 'am I, thus to lie in this horrible dungeon, when I may as well walk at liberty. I have a key in my bosom called promise, that will, I am persuaded, open any lock in Doubting Castle.' Then said Hopeful, 'That's good news, good brother; pluck it out of thy bosom and try.' Then Christian pulled it out of his bosom, and began to try the dungeon door, whose bolts gave back and the door flew open with ease and Christian and Hopeful came out."   *Bunyan's Pilgrim's Progress.*

If any door closes it is only that God is opening a larger one.

. . . After He had offered one sacrifice for sins forever, (He) sat down on the right hand of God; from henceforth expecting . . . (Heb. 10:12, 13).

> He expecteth, He expecteth! Down the stream of time
> Still the words come softly ringing like a chime.
> Ofttimes faint, now waxing louder, as the hour draws near
> When the King in all His glory shall appear.
>
> He is waiting with long patience for His crowning day,
> For that Kingdom which shall never pass away,
> And till every tribe and nation bow before His throne,
> He expecteth loyal service from His own.
>
> He expecteth—but He heareth still the bitter cry
> From earth's millions, "Come and help us for we die."
> He expecteth—doth He see us busy here and there,
> Heedless of those pleading accents of despair?
>
> Shall we—dare we disappoint Him? Brethren let us rise!
> He who died for us is watching from the skies;
> Watching till His royal banner floateth far and wide,
> Till He seeth of His travail satisfied!

After twenty centuries, one billion heathen have never heard the greatest story ever told. At whose door lieth this sin?

It is good for me that I have been afflicted that I might learn thy statutes (Psalm 119:71).

In "Fanny Crosby's Life Story of Herself," this remarkable statement of faith in God's overruling hand of Providence appears: "I have heard that this physician (who unwittingly caused her blindness), never ceased to express his regret at the occurrence; and that it was one of the sorrows of his life. But if I could meet him now, I would say, 'Thank you, thank you, over and over again, for making me blind . . . ' Although it may have been a blunder on the physician's part, it was no mistake on God's. I verily believe it was His intention that I should live my days in physical darkness, so as to be better prepared to sing His praises and incite others so to do."

Fanny Crosby, blind writer of six thousand hymns testified, "I am the happiest creature in all the land."

> O what a happy soul am I
>   Although I cannot see,
> I am resolved that in this world
>   Contented I will be;
> How many blessings I enjoy
>   That other people don't,
> To weep and sigh because I'm blind,
>   I cannot and I won't.

Written by Fanny Crosby at the age of eight.

For Thou hast been a strength to the poor, a strength to the needy in his distress, a refuge from the storm, a shadow from the heat when the blast of the terrible ones is as a storm against the wall (Isa. 25:4).

Lord make me strong! Let my soul rooted be
   Afar from vales of rest,
   Flung close to heaven upon a great Rock's breast,
Unsheltered and alone, but strong in Thee.

What though the lashing tempests leave their scars?
   Has not the Rock been bruised?
   Mine, with the strength of ages deep infused,
To face the storms and triumph with the stars!

Lord, plant my spirit high upon the crest
   Of Thine eternal strength!
   Then though life's breaking struggles come at length
Their storms shall only bend me to Thy breast.

Dorothy Clarke Wilson.

Trees that brave storms are not propagated in hothouses.

For there is hope of a tree if it be cut down that it will sprout again and that the tender branch thereof will not cease. Though the root thereof wax old in the earth, and the stock thereof die in the ground; yet through the scent of water it will bud and bring forth boughs like a plant (Job 14:7-9).

The famous grapevine at Hampton Court, England is probably the largest in the world. As the keeper was telling how many thousand clusters it bore, I said to him that the grapes seemed very small for Black Hamburgs. "Yes," he said, "an old vine bears as large grapes and clusters as a younger one; but the grapes are sweeter and of finer flavor. They are kept for the Queen's use."

It is true, and it is a comfort, that with the lesser quantities of fruit old age can bear for the Lord, the quality of the fruit may be better, and the flavor more heavenly.

Let us not be weary in well doing, for in due season we shall reap if we faint not (Gal. 6:9).

I t is the last step that wins; and there is no place in the pilgrim's progress where so many dangers lurk as the region that lies hard by the portals of the Celestial City. It was there that Doubting Castle stood. It was there that the enchanted ground lured the tired traveler to fatal slumber.

It is when Heaven's heights are in full view that hell's gate is most persistent and full of deadly peril.

> In the bitter waves of woe
>   Beaten and tossed about
> By the sullen winds that blow
>   From the desolate shores of doubt,
> Where the anchors that faith has cast
>   Are dragging in the gale,
> I am quietly holding fast
>   To the things that cannot fail.
>
> And fierce though the fiends may fight,
>   And long though the angels hide,
> I know that truth and right
>   Have the universe on their side;
> And that somewhere beyond the stars
>   Is a love that is better than fate.
> When the night unlocks her bars
>   I shall see Him—I will wait.   *Washington Gladden.*

. . . Trust . . . in the living God who giveth us richly all things to enjoy (1 Tim. 6:17).

A story is told of Mrs. Spurgeon who had been an invalid for years. She had been wishing that she might have a canary. She had told no one about her desire—not even her husband—but she did lay the matter before the Lord, believing that He would, without her telling anyone about it, send her a bird to cheer her sick room.

One day when Mr. Spurgeon came home she told him that some anonymous friend had sent her a beautiful canary—there it was, cage and all! She said, "I have been asking God to send me a bird."

Her husband replied, "I think you are one of the Lord's spoiled children; you get whatever you ask for."

God not only gives His children raiment to wear and food to eat, but He can give them luxuries. And what a wealth of spiritual luxuries too, the God of Heaven is waiting to shower upon His children in answer to prayer.

As for me, I will behold thy face in righteousness. I shall be satisfied when I awake with thy likeness (Psalm 17:15).

D o not feel sorry for me, brethren," said a minister to his fellow-pastors as he was accepting retired relationship at a conference. "The end of my days here is not sunset for me, but sunrise! You see, the end of this life is not death, but resurrection unto eternal life; not crying but rejoicing, not a funeral, but a festival. If God should call me Home, it would be but the beginning of life eternal. You have the wrong emphasis when you speak of my having reached the sunset time of life. I am walking steadily into the sunrise of tomorrow."

There is no sunset to a Christian's life; it is the dawn of a fadeless glory—no sunset, but the breaking of God's eternal day.

. . . They went everyone straight forward (Ezek. 10:22).

E dwin Markham, the great poet, at eighty wrote a poem entitled "The Look Ahead."

> I am done with the years that were,
>   I am quits;
> I am done with the dead and old
>   They are mines worked out,
>   I delved in their pits;
> I have saved their grain of gold.
>
> Now I trun to the future for wine and bread;
> I have bidden the past adieu.
> I laugh and lift hands to the years ahead;
> "Come on, I am ready for you."

Dear God of all ages and the ageless, help those of us who are young to thank Thee for all that life holds for us, and those of us who are older grown, to thank Thee for the immortality that unfolds before us in the heavenly reaches. In Thy blessed name, Amen.

And when he putteth forth his own sheep, he goeth before them and the sheep follow him; for they know his voice (John 10:4).

Dr. A. J. Gossip, the great gifted Scottish preacher tells of a pleasant experience one day in France.

He had been for weeks amid the appalling desolation and sickening sights of the war front. Then they had gone back to rest where there were budding hedgerows, a shimmer of green on living trees, grass and flowers—flowers glorious in the first splendor of spring. It seemed Heaven! Then came the order to return to Passchendaele and the battle front.

"It reached us," said Dr. Gossip, "on a perfect afternoon of sunshine; and with a heart grown hot and hard, I turned down a little lane with a brown burn whimpling beside it, and a lush meadow—all brave sheets of purple and golden flowers—on either side. The earth was very beautiful and life seemed very sweet and it was hard to go back into the old purgatory and face death again.

"With that, through the gap in the hedge there came a shepherd laddie, tending his flock of some two dozen sheep. He was not driving them in our rough way with two barking dogs: he went first and they were following him; if one loitered, he called it by name and it came running to him. So they moved on down the lane, up a little hill, up to the brow and over it, and so out of my life.

"Then, I turned and went down the lane to face what was to be, with a heart quieted and stilled."

_____

They shall still bring forth fruit in old age; they shall be full of sap and green (Psalm 92:14—RV).

I n the secluded garden of Christ's College, at Cambridge, there is a mulberry tree of which tradition says that it was planted by John Milton in his student days.

I remember sitting on the green turf below it, a few years ago, and looking up at the branches, heavy with age and propped on crutches, and wondering to see that the old tree still brought forth fruit. It was not the size nor the quality of the fruit that impressed me. I hardly thought of that. *The strange thing, the beautiful thing, was that after so many years, the tree was yet bearing.*

Henry Van Dyke.

. . . Called to be saints . . . (1 Cor. 1:2).

Why were the saints, saints?
It is quite simple.
Because they were cheerful
When it was difficult to be cheerful.
Patient, when it was difficult to be patient.
Because they pushed on
When they wanted to stand still.
And kept silent
When they wanted to talk.
And were agreeable when they wanted to be disagreeable.
That was all!

Saintliness will not protect you from senselessness.

. . . Moses wist not that the skin of his face shone . . . (Exod. 34:29).

Henry Drummond in addressing an assembly of women said, "After you have been kind—after love has stolen forth into the world and done its beautiful work, go back into the shade again and say nothing about it."

I once heard Rendel Harris say of the Bible critics, "They may tear the volume to shreds, but they can never rub off the light of God from the faces of His people."

It was seraphic Murray McCheyne who said, "Oh, for the holy shining of the face! and oh, for the holy ignorance of the shining."

An old woman opened a conversation with a man on a trolley car. "Are you a minister of religion?" she asked.

"No," he said with a smile, "but why do you ask?"

"Because, sir, you have a Bible face."

Robert Louis Stevenson asked God to forgive him if he had not shown "a morning face."

. . . The dayspring (sunrising, marg.) from on high hath visited us (Luke 1:78).

Have you ever watched the dawn as it slowly and gradually develops until it becomes day? I have, and one special time of watching it is deeply engraven on my memory. It was midsummer night in Sweden, and I stayed up looking out of my window until twelve o'clock. As that hour was striking I opened my Bible, and by the glow of the western sky read the twenty-first chapter of the Book of Revelation which contains that wonderful description of the New Jerusalem, culminating in the words, "There shall be no night there." Scarcely could it be called "night" there in Sweden—only two hours of semi-darkness between sunset and sunrise, but the "no night" of the new heaven and earth means much more than this earthly absence of night. No night of sorrow, for "God shall wipe away all tears from their eyes"; no night of death for death shall be "swallowed up in victory."

I went to bed then without having had to use artificial light. I awoke at three, and got up to see the dawn. Oh, how still and hushed it was! It was as though God had said, "Let there be peace!" and there was peace. A great calm lay upon everything.

The waters of the island-studded lake had not a single ripple on their surface; they were as a "sea of glass," while nature all around—the opposite wooded shore, and the nearer rocky and richly vegetated isles—seemed silent with a great expectation and anticipation. The sky was clear and blue, without the hint of a cloud. The morning star shone in the south, while in the east there was a faint promise of day!

It was utterly unearthly-looking, and more as if one had got a sudden and beautiful glimpse of Heaven! He has come once, our Morning Star in deep humiliation, as a despised and rejected One; He is coming again with great glory—*"His coming is as certain as the Dawn!"*

We believe and are sure that thou art the Christ, the Son of the living God (John 6:69).

When Benjamin Franklin was dying, someone asked him what was the nature of his speculations now.

He replied, "I am not speculating. I am not resting my dying head on a pillow of guesswork. I know whom I have believed."

> Before the Throne my surety stands,
> My name is written on His hands!

"I know that Christ is because I talked with Him this morning," said *Bishop Thoburn, veteran missionary of the cross.*

. . . Take root downward, and bear fruit upward (2 Kings 19:30).

S ome months ago, in the late autumn, the writer was in the hothouse of one of our florists. We were in the cellar, and in the dimly lighted place, one could see arranged in regular file, long rows of flower pots. The florist explained that in these pots had been planted the bulbs for their winter flowers. It was best for them that they be rooted in the dark. Not in the glaring sunlight, but in the subdued shadows, their life-giving roots were putting forth. They would be ready for the open day a little later. Then their gay colors would cheer many hearts. Then their sweet perfumes would laden the winter air. Rooted in the shadows to bloom in the light! Roots then roses.

The strongest plants begin with unseen roots.

It matters little where our life is lived or what kind of weather we meet, if our roots are finding the eternal springs.

Wrote a Persian poet: *"How shall my leaves fly singing in the wind unless my roots shall wither in the dark?"*

The things which are impossible with men are possible with God (Luke 18:27).

>   Canst thou take the barren soil
>   And with all thy pains and toil
>   Make lilies blow?
>   Thou canst not. O helpless man,
>   Have faith in God—He can.
>
>   Canst thou paint the clouds at eve?
>   And all the sunset colors weave
>   Into the sky?
>   Thou canst not. O powerless man,
>   Have faith in God—He can.
>
>   Canst thou still thy troubled heart
>   And make all cares and doubts depart
>   From out thy soul?
>   Thou canst not. O faithless man,
>   Have faith in God—He can.

Thy God will accomplish all that thy faith has laid on Him.

Upon Simon, a Cyrenian . . . they laid the cross that he might bear it after Jesus (Luke 23:26).

A rchibald Rutledge, author of "Old Plantation Days" and "Children of the Swamp and Wood," says "I never knew a Negro atheist or free-thinker. The Negro race is by instinct religious. Out of its heart has issued the Negro spirituals, one of the two types of genuine lyrics."

Is there not something strange in the fact that it was a representative of Africa who bore the hinder part of the cross with Jesus? Cyrene was a powerful city of Africa. Simon was a colored man. Mark tells us that he had two sons, one of whom is believed to be the Rufus mentioned by Paul as "chosen in the Lord." Wherever the black man has since come to know the Gospel, he has manifested a depth of feeling not often found in other races and he had been a great cross-bearer.

With pathetically little to give of things material, they are spendthrifts of heart—which is perhaps life's final wisdom.

Say unto the peoples; the Lord reigneth from the tree (Psalm 96:10—Latin).

At the time of the Crucifixion, the dogwood tree was as large and strong as the oak, and was chosen as the timber for the Cross.

To be used for this purpose distressed the tree, and Jesus, in His pity, promised: "Never again shall you grow large enough to be used for a cross. Henceforth the dogwood tree shall be slender and twisted; its blossoms in the form of a cross . . . two long and two short petals. At the edge of each petal there shall be nail prints; in the center of the flower, a crown of thorns. And this tree shall be cherished as a reminder of my Cross."

So it has been, and the springtime flowering of the dogwood has remained a symbol of divine sacrifice and the triumph of eternal life.

> When on the cross My Lord did bleed
> Life seemed to die, death died indeed.

Wherefore God also hath highly exalted Him . . . (Phil. 2:9).

The descent of our Lord into the sphere of time and sense is a solemn fact to be celebrated with wonder and gratitude, but His exaltation is because of all his ransomed worshippers.

The crown of thorns glows into gold and multiplies into diadems; the marred face makes the sun dim; the pierced hand grasps the universal sceptre; the cross towers and expands with a throne based on the jasper and girded by the rainbow.

Do we think enough, anything like enough, of the royalty of our Master? In all the days when we have the sense of impatience and struggle, let us remember whose we are and whom we serve. We need a fresh sense of the Fatherhood of God; the profound heart-comfort of it.

"I hold the world in my hand, but I can also hold you," saith our Lord.

The love of Christ constraineth us . . . (2 Cor. 5:14).

The only real mystery of the Bible, according to an old writer, is the mystery of love. God so loved the world as to give His only begotten Son. What! That for a lost and ruined world, the Prince of Life should leave the bosom on which He had been pillowed from all eternity and expire by an ignominious death on the bitter tree! Love unutterable! Limitless! Infinite majesty compassioning infinite weakness!

Man never can get farther in the solution of the wondrous problem. Eternity itself will form a ladder—the saints climbing step by step in its ascending glories, but as the prospect widens, each new altitude will elicit the same confession, "The love of Christ which passeth knowledge!"

God's measureless measure—Love!

Capture the waves from a thousand oceans,
Mix with the songs of a million birds;
Fathom the depths of a heart's emotions;
Measure the power of spoken words;
Condense the perfume of a billion flowers;
Pluck every gleam from the stars above;
Blend all with the joy of a trillion hours
And express one atom of infinite love!

He shall see of the travail of his soul and shall be satisfied . . . (Isa. 53:11).

A waiting Christ! Waiting! For what? For whom? Has Calvary failed? Never! A hating world nailed our Saviour to the cross of shame, but they lifted him up only that He might draw all men unto Him! His cross of thorns became a diadem of royalty. The cross was a symbol of conquest and glory. And now, the fullness of the time has come—the age-end before His return.

"This gospel of the kingdom shall be preached in all the world . . . and then shall the end come."

We stand on the threshold of the most marvelous hour of all history! 'Tis the grandest hour for God since morning stars sang together at creation's dawn. The whole world is thrilling to the name of Jesus as never before. This is the hour.

> He is waiting with long patience,
>   For His crowning day,
> For that Kingdom which shall never
>   Pass away.

O wounded hand, grasp the sceptre! O thorn-pierced brow, wear the crown! O pierced feet, mount the throne!

T. Dewitt Talmadge

I am he that liveth and was dead, and behold, I am alive forevermore, Amen . . . (Rev. 1:18).

A new dawn broke with the sweet glory of spring, the music of bird-song, the fragrance of lilies, and in the first rays of that morning light, troubled women found an open tomb. A messenger in white spoke the most glorious word ever uttered to mankind: "He is not here! He is risen!"

"Because I live ye shall live also." We shall have our Easter morn, by the same divine power. Of us, too, it shall be said, "He is not here!" This is our faith; this is the great hope of Easter morning.

Faith wipes away her tears on Easter day. For on Easter day, faith hastens early in the morning to an empty tomb. No sorrowful inscription tells her that "here lies the Son of God."

"Where is Kanderstag?" a traveler in Switzerland asked a lad along the road. "I do not know where Kanderstag is," replied the lad, "but there's the road that leads to it." *I do not know where life hereafter is, but Easter Dawn is the road that leads to it.*

And having spoiled principalities and powers, he made a show of them openly, triumphing over them in it (Col. 2:15).

I feel a tingling to the tips of my fingers and through every nerve of my body and the depths of my soul—an earnest of our ultimate triumph. Cheer up, O men and women! Pitch your tents toward the sunrising! *F. Daniel Talmadge.*

When Christ died, His cry, "It is finished!" was the triumphant proclamation of His victory over all the powers of sin, hell and death. Since then, all who accept personally, the victory of the Cross, experience a new power over sin and temptation, over disappointments, trials and fears. Even death loses its dreaded sting. There is victory in the Cross; it "towers o'er the wrecks of time," in our individual lives.

The resurrection is God's "Amen" to Christ's "It is Finished."

And if Christ be not raised, your faith is vain; ye are yet in your sins . . . but now is Christ risen from the dead and become the firstfruits of them that slept (1 Cor. 15:17, 20).

The resurrection of Christ is the need of our day. He has dwelt behind a curtain of mysticism; He has been buried in the grave of ecclesiastical formulae, wrapped about by the cerements of superstition, until the common people who would hear him gladly if he were permitted to speak the language of their common life have grown weary and sad, saying, "They have taken away my Lord, and I know not where they have laid Him."

Frances Willard.

The resurrection is God's receipt in full to Jesus Christ for the sin debt of the whole world.

Behold my hands and my feet, that it is I myself . . . (Luke 24:39).

From the time of our Lord's resurrection even until today, the human spirit that is seeking earnestly for God has been able to recognize the presence of the living Christ. It is as true today as it was in the days of Christ that "faith has still its Olivet and love its Galilee."

The reader of the Holy Scriptures is ever intrigued by Christ's identification of Himself to His disciples and by their recognition of His living presence.

Today it is for us, just as it was for the eleven, to hear Him say, "It is I myself." It is for us, as it was for Cleopas and his friend at Emmaus, to know Him. It is for us, as it was for Mary Magdalene, to catch our breath and cry, "Rabboni!"

It is for us, as for Thomas, to exclaim in all humility, "My Lord and my God." Yes, "faith has still its Olivet and love its Galilee," for we "meet Him in life's throng and press" and in every devotional experience of life, and we are "whole again."

Today I will watch and listen for Him who goeth before me into all of life.

For I am the Lord, I change not . . . (Mal. 3:6).

By the door of an old farmhouse in Connecticut there grows a white lilac bush, lifting its perfumed plumes in the spring air, sturdy and strong whatever winds may blow. The people who planted it went to heaven many a long year ago, and the gray-haired couple who occupied the house when last I saw it are safe amid the fadeless gardens above. But the same flowers come back year after year, preaching the same sweet sermon of the changeless faithfulness of our God.

When the last Easter music has melted away into space, when the Easter garlands are withered, and from the mount of our Easter exaltation, we descend to the valleys and the common-places of our daily lives, let this be our ceaseless joy: that God is ever with us. Always the same Gospel. He, who year in, year out, sends the shower and the sunbeam, dresses highway and byway with beauty, from the dogwood to the goldenrod, from the green leaf to the brown, will not forget the least of us. *His goodness is ever new; His kindness always outpoured, His tenderness greater than our uttermost demand, and the same springtime over and over is sent by the same dear Lord and Father.*

. . . One day with the Lord is as a thousand years . . . (2 Peter 3:8).

> One poor day!
> > Remember whose and how short it is.
> > It is God's day; it is Columbus'.
> > One day with life and heart is more than time enough
> > > to found a world.   *James Russell Lowell*

For the road winds uphill all the way to the end, and the journey takes the whole day long, from morn till night.

Morning never yet has failed when night is through.

And I will give thee the treasures of darkness, and hidden riches of secret places, that thou mayest know that I, the Lord, which call thee by thy name am . . . God . . . (Isa. 45:3).

One of the first questions that came to my mind after the black curtain of blindness fell over my eyes was: "What can the Lord do with a blind man?" For long ago I had given myself to the service of the Lord, and had undergone long years of training for my work as a minister. I tried every known means to halt the degeneration of the eye tissue, but all to no avail. The thing I had dreaded did happen; and the day came when I had to admit that I could not longer see and the doctor pronounced me totally and permanently blind.

That was a black day for me, and darker than the mantle that covered my eyes was the mental and spiritual blackout that overwhelmed my mind and soul.

I wrestled in prayer and meditation and I found a new sense of peace and power. I tried often during my sleepless hours to repeat portions from the Scriptures, and I learned how to pray as I had never prayed before. The time came when I no longer dreaded wakefulness, for I found rest and peace and confidence through communion with God as I lay upon my bed. Thus I came to discover the treasures of darkness.

I determined to make the most of each day and fill it full of courage and cheerfulness. I realized that others who had to live with me had a right to be happy and I must not rob them of their happiness, simply because I was afflicted. Neither should the fact that I had a handicap serve to rob me of my happiness nor keep me from finding help and strength and faith to carry on.

I have no time to be sorry for myself. I do not feel that the days of my usefulness are over, but I have the hope that my best days are yet ahead of me. I live in the darkness, but I do not live alone. *There walks One with me Who is able to make even the darkness light about me, and by the light of His presence I have discovered the unsearchable riches of Christ, the treasures of darkness and it is God my Maker Who giveth me songs in the night.*

And the gates of it shall not be shut at all by day; for there shall be no night there (Rev. 21:25).

Where is Heaven? God's Word tells us in Revelation 22:1-6 and John 14:1, 2.

Our God of infinite love could not build that mansion for you in another way than by using His own nail-pierced hands, and cementing it together with His own heart's blood. He is preparing the place where no east wind blows and no hailstone falls, and where there is no sorrow and never a sigh.

It is there, weary traveler, that they count not time by years.

And when on that last day we rise,
Caught up between the earth and skies,
    Then shall we hear our Lord
Say, Thou hast done with doubt and death,
Henceforth, according to thy faith,
    Shall be thy faith's reward.

P. C.

What is man that thou are mindful of him? and the son of man that thou visitest him? For thou hast made him a little lower than the angels and hast crowned him with glory and honor (Psalm 8:4-5).

When you get discouraged with yourself, remember that God made you. Look at your finger tips. None others in all the world carved in delicate lines like yours are hands carved by God Himself.

Who but a God of infinite skill, intelligence and experience, could ever have made your eyes, with all their delicate nerves, lenses and light curtains? Who but a living God could have given you such senses, capable of bringing in such beauty and surprise?

Who keeps your heart going so steadily and so dependably? Who orders all the strange chemical reactions that go on in your digestive tract? Who stays on the job while you are asleep, keeping things in order?

R. L. S.

My great concern is not whether God is on our side, my great concern is to be on God's side. Abraham Lincoln.

. . . Singing and making melody in your heart to the Lord (Eph. 5:19).

Singing will clear the sky of clouds almost as if by magic. Work is made of joy when one goes about it singing. Songs are contagious. As everybody loves a lover, so everybody enjoys folks whose gladness bursts forth in song. Singing is one of God's richest gifts to man.

A messenger-boy ran up the steps of a home singing, "Brighten the corner where you are," and the lady who was sweeping off her porch was soon singing that melody. The woman next door took it up and was singing it, when finally down the street it went, on wings of gladness. All because a plain messenger boy gave vent to the joybells of life.

> Tell Him about your heartache
> And tell Him your loneliness too,
> Tell Him your baffled purpose
> When you scarce know what to do.
> Then leaving all your weakness
> With the One divinely strong,
> Forget that you bear the burden
> And carry away the song.

Many people endure their religion more than they enjoy it.

All thy works praise thee, O Lord . . . (Psalm 145:10).

At a wayside shack just off a highway where we once stopped to inquire directions, a wistful looking woman, drawn into conversation, said, "We don't have any music, we haven't a radio, and we don't get to town. I wish I was you-all." Behind the shack there was a little pond where, in the shade of overhanging willows, some ducks drifted lazily. "Have you any frogs in your pond?" I inquired, and she said indifferently, "Yes, and they croak every night."

In my hillside garden the frogs have a choral which I would not exchange for any other. When twilight comes the big basso tunes up, directs and leads, and soon the woodland music of a score of lusty throats take up the symphony, deep and tuneful, in a manner peculiar to frogs. To me this is one of the night's loveliest sounds. Often we silence the radio, which we enjoy in its way, to get the quivering chorus of the little brown and green choristers of the pool. There is no other music like it. At dawning the twittering and calling of the birds awakens the sleeper. During the day the gladsome note of the feathered songsters is heard over the garden.

This poor deaf woman had let her ears be tuned to the horizon, and never knew that she was missing the wonderful harmonies of nature. Just as so often we fix our eyes on the "apples on the other side of the wall."

Of course it was lonesome without music. Anyone will appreciate that. But, when I asked her about frogs and bees she said, "Doz you get anything out of that?" I replied, "Yes, I've brought them in all the way from the country just to hear their music." Then I asked her to listen and she had a new vision of the music about her. *Carrie Jacobs Bond.*

In this hurried world, would it not be well for us to take a little time now and again to listen to the melodies. Why not hear a sky-tune now and then?

There is plenty of heavenly music for those who have tuned in.

Ye are our epistle written in our hearts, known and read of all men (2 Cor. 3:2).

There is no finer offering that we can give to the world, than that we should give character stamped with the image of God, that we should be men and women in whom God lives and in whom God is forming Himself.

The wife of Dr. Andrew Bonar was led to the Lord by the saintly McCheyne whose life has been an inspiration to multitudes. Mrs. Bonar always said, "It was not his matter or his manner that impressed me, but it was just the living epistle of Christ—a picture so lovely that I would have given the world to be such as he is."

A minister in the north of Scotland met McCheyne and was in his presence for a little while. He said he never met a more Jesus-like man in the world and he went into his room to weep and pray and give himself to God.

Oh, to be like Thee, Blessed Redeemer!

> Truth beyond my comprehension
> Fact with which I'll never part;
> Though I'm but an "earthen vessel"
> I have Jesus in my heart.
> Oh the joy to know it's true!
> He himself said, "I in you."

. . . Lo, I am with you all the appointed days (Matt. 28:20—Variorum Version).

I fear no more the coming years
   What they may bring.
Days will be sunless, nights bereft of stars;
   Mayhap the brightest blossoms of the Spring
Shall first be bound with winter's icy bars.
But still beyond the cloud is always light,
The stars are in the sky all night,
And deepest snows are they which hide the bright
   Green heart of Spring.

God's smile shines where the path goes winding forever, and every turn in the road brings new blessedness.

. . . God meant it unto good . . . (Gen. 50:20).

Trouble is a blessing; it brings out—it rough-hews us—and its repeated blows chisel us into fair proportions and beauty. Endure, be tested, tried and proven, rejoice and be glad. Trouble becomes triumph if rightly used. Rejoice in the midst of trouble. Be calm, still, quiet. Rest in Him.

Let the troubles work; don't hinder, never complain. Stillness is the way to take trouble; count it all joy. Let your heart beat so you can hear it, and it is surely out of order; let your brain buzz and brain disease will ensue. Fret and worry about trouble and you are out of condition.

We shall look some day with wonder at the troubles we have had.

When God ploughs, He intends to sow.

Their office was to . . . stand every morning to thank and praise the Lord, and likewise at even (1 Chron. 23:28, 30).

I heard a bluebird in the field today,
   Shouting aloud its springtime joy;
My heart leaped backward through the years
   And knelt before a laughing boy.

"Oh boy, " I pray, "give back to me
   My laughter of that other day;
Give me the spirit, glad and free,
   That once I knew along the way."

He saw me not! Yet in his eye
   I read the answer to my plea;
"Joy lives not in the yesterdays,
   But in the living now," said he.

"Seize thou the joy of every day,
   For gladness thrills the common sod,
And every brook and every bird
   May sing to you the joy of God."

Joy is the flag which flies from the castle of the heart when the King is in residence there.

. . . Moses drew near unto the thick darkness where God was (Exod. 20:21).

How pleasant the sound as the raindrops patter against the window pane and say a cheery, "Good day!" Did you ever see the raindrops come when there were no clouds? Clouds are God's receptacles and harbingers of blessing in nature. Yet, they shut out the sun, cover the moon and stars and shorten the horizon. What blessings they bring—a softened and mellowed earth, growth and fruition of crops.

Often we foolishly wish that all our days would be bright and clear. Then when the clouds come we become discouraged and fearful. We fail to realize that the dark clouds of afflictions and trials are but God's vehicles of blessings sent to soften and mellow our hearts and make them fruitful and useful for Him. Remember, God sees right through the thick cloud and watches and cares for His own. Trust Him and be of good cheer.

Trust is never tension; true faith is complete relaxation.

_____

It matters to Him about you (1 Peter 5:7—RV).

A policeman was holding up the busy traffic with his white gloved hands. The automobiles and taxis all stood obedient; the boys on bicycles put one foot to the ground and held onto whatever was nearest to them; all the work of that busy street was stopped. All the people wondered who could be coming, and many craned their necks to see if it were the King of England about to drive through the big gates of the Palace.

Then came a surprise indeed! On the empty street, so carefully guarded and protected, there walked across, looking very proud and clever, a mother duck with her ten little ducklings in single file behind her! There they waddled—all the little necks on a stretch, all the little beaks a-twitter, all the little eyes wide open. When they got safely across, the big policeman lowered his arm and the waves of traffic surged on once more.

Relax, Christian, lean your whole weight on the Lord. He will never let you down.

Remember the word unto thy servant which thou hast caused me to hope (Psalm 119:49).

After the autumn leaf there is the spring leaf. No intervention of winter, no wild calling of the winter winds disturb us. If we love Christ we run out of the shadows to the glory and the beauty of the eternal springtime, where flowers are eternal and the springtime clouds glory along the sky.

> I wonder how I ever could have wept
> Last autumn when I watched the flying leaves come down,
> Each leaf a promise of a swift return
> After the barren months, wearing her verdant gown.
> Oh, why will mortals take so long to learn
> That laughter follows after winter rain?
> Spring will return again!   *Ruth Margaret Gibbs.*

Faith sees crowns growing on the top of crosses.

. . . I will see you again and your heart will rejoice . . . (John 16:22).

A traveler chanced on a beautiful villa, situated on the shores of a beautiful lake in Switzerland, far from the beaten track of tourists. He knocked at the garden gate, and an aged gardener unlocked its heavy fastenings and bade him enter. The aged man seemed glad to see him and showed him around the wonderful garden.

"How long have you been here?" the traveler asked.

"Twenty-four years."

"How often has your master been here meanwhile? When was he here last?"

"Twelve years ago."

"He writes often?"

"Never once."

"From whom do you receive your pay?"

"His agent in the mainland."

"But he comes here often?"

"He has never been here."

"Who does come then?"

"I am almost always alone; it is very, very seldom that even a stranger comes."

"Yet, you have the garden in such perfect order, everything flourishing, as if you were expecting your master's coming tomorrow."

"As if he were coming today, sir, today!" exclaimed the old man.

. . . He giveth his beloved sleep (Psalm 127:2).

L oss of sleep will never be missed if we spend the time in communion with the Master. He changes our attitude toward the things we fear, helps us forgive where forgiveness is necessary, and puts love into our hearts for those who irritate and annoy us. It is the worries and anxieties that make us tired and drive away our sleep—not long hours of work or a weary body. There is no one like the Lord for smoothing out the worries and stilling the anxious thoughts.

> The world is wide
> In time and tide,
> And God is Guide;
>   Then do not hurry.
>
> That man is blest
> Who does his best
> And leaves the rest;
>   Then do not worry.

Charles F. Deems.

Thou hast not always promised me rest from my burden, but Thou hast always offered me rest in my burden.

George Matheson.

But made himself of no reputation and took upon him the form of a servant, and was made in the likeness of men (Phil. 2:7).

C hrist took the crooked and made it straight. He turned the waste places into fruitful fields; briars into myrtle; thorns into roses; the wind-blown deserts of shifting sands into the gardens of God. He put laughter on the lip, light into the sightless eye, faith in the heart of fear, and set the star of hope on the black bosom of the night of sin and death. He shattered the night with the morning light. He made visible to sight the unseen God, pulled aside the curtains of time, and revealed forever the gleaming towers and marble halls in the yonder land beside the tideless sea. He rebuilt the fires of faith in human hearts and set earth and ages ablaze with God.

> He might have built a palace at a word
> Who sometimes had not where to lay His head;
> Time was when He who nourished crowds with bread
> Would not one meal unto Himself afford.
> Twelve legions girded with angelic sword
> Were at His beck—the scorned and buffeted.
> He healed another's scratch; His own side bled,
> Side, feet, hands with cruel piercings gored.
> Oh, wonderful, the wonders left undone.
> And scarce less wonderful than those He wrought.
> Oh, self restraint passing all human thought,
> Lo, have all power and be as having none.
> Oh, self denying love, which felt alone
> For needs of others, never for its own.

True consecration knows no reservations.

When thou passeth through the waters . . . they shall not overflow thee . . . (Isa. 43:2).

When Mrs. Booth, the mother of the Salvation Army, one of God's great warriors, had reached the silver river where bright angel feet were treading, waiting to carry her over into the land of pure delight where saints immortal reign, where everlasting day excludes the night and pleasures banish fear, where everlasting spring abides and never fading flowers, she said quietly, "The waters are rising, but I am not sinking."

Why could she say that? Was it not because she had been saying that all her life? Other floods besides death had gathered about her soul. Often her road was deep in affliction. She had never sunk. She rode upon the storm, for she rested upon the promises of her Lord. It is the promises that make us buoyant.

God does not promise that waters of trouble shall never gather about His children, but He does make it possible for them to keep their heads above water. Dr. Jowett calls it "the grace of aboveness." *God's children shall never be under the circumstances—always above!*

He hath made everything beautiful in its time . . . (Eccl. 3:11—RV).

Through the crisp autumn morning the sunlight streams, jeweling each fog-tipped blade and leaf. A girl comes swiftly down the path, her cheeks pink, her hair wind-tossed about her face and her wide eyes alight with hope and faith.

Quickly she glances over the landscape which seems to be giving itself to the last caress of summer.

"O, this beautiful world!" she says joyously, and her mouth curves up in a smile of happiness. "I am so glad I am here and that the long years stretch out before me in which to live and love."

The noonday sun by its kisses has dried the leaves and grass as it poured in a stream of gold down the hillside path and rested in the eyes of the woman as she looks into the tender smile of the man beside her.

All the joy of life is in their glances; all the bliss of love is on their lips. Her hands seek his as her gaze wanders to the horizon and comes back to rest upon his face.

"Oh, this beautiful world!" she whispers as she leans her head against his heart. "I am so glad I am here—here close beside you, living and loving."

The early darkness of the gathering twilight comes creeping fast. Gone are the dream diamonds of the morning; gone the real gold of the noonday.

A woman lingers alone in the path by the garden gate. There are strands of white in her hair, and her weary eyes peer almost wistfully through the deepening shadows as though she would gladly lay down life's burdens and walk beyond.

But as her trembling hands swing back the portal, she turns once more to the pathway which is now molten silver in the moonlight. To her comes white-robed memory with glorified face and outstretched arms.

"Oh, this beautiful world!" the woman murmurs. *"I am so thankful that it has been my lot to have lived and loved."*

Ida McGlone Gibson.

He shall cover thee with his feathers, and under His wings shalt thou trust . . . (Psalm 91:4).

There are four calls by which the hen calls in her brood. The first is the call of night, when they need a shelter from the dampness and from the darkness. The second is the call for food, when the hen would attract her little ones to pick up some dainty morsel that she has found for them. The third is the call of danger, when the hawk descends, or the brood is in peril. And the fourth is the call of love, when, with motherly desire and yearning, she would gather her brood where they may feel the softness of her breast-feathers and the warmth of her own body.

When the night shadows are falling, when the night hawk is descending, when food is needed by you in your hunger, or when my love yearns for a closer embrace, you *shall find a safe and delightful shelter under the shadow of My wings.* A. T. Pierson.

Ye are my friends . . . (John 15:14).

I suppose that the greatest title ever conferred upon men was the one used by Jesus when He addressed His disciples as "my Friends." Compared with this, all other titles and nobilities are tawdry and artificial. They are as wax flowers and fruits in contrast with the sweet-perfumed loveliness of gardens and woods. They are like harsh, glaring stage effects set in contrast with the soft splendors of the dawn. An earthly dignity always carries with it a certain autumnal air, a suggestion of the fading leaf. The heavenly dignity is always significant of the eternal spring. "My Friends." No other honor will ever come our way which for a moment can be compared to this.   *J.H. Jowett.*

"Tell me, dear, if your mother is a widow and so poor that she cannot afford to rent a comfortable place to live in, what is it that makes her so happy?"

"I don't know," said the child musingly, "unless, it is because God is her friend."

Many daughters have done virtuously but thou excellest them all (Prov. 31:29).

Only a woman! In the thirty years of my married life, I have served 255,425 meals, made 33,190 loaves of bread, 5,930 cakes and 7,960 pies. I have canned 1,550 quarts of fruit, raised 7,660 chickens, churned 5,540 pounds of butter, put in 36,461 hours sweeping, washing, scrubbing. I estimate the worth of my labor conservatively at $115,485.50 none of which I have ever collected. But I still love my husband and children and wouldn't mind starting all over again for them!"

Whenever they start voting to fill the niches in the Hall of Fame, we cannot help thinking of a number of women like that. It is among such wives and mothers that you will find the real uncrowned queens of earth!

A Mother's love is a fire that burns and is not consumed; it is something inexhaustible.

. . . A woman that feareth the Lord, she shall be praised. Give her of the fruit of her hands; and let her own works praise her in the gates (Prov. 31:30, 31).

On summer eves when purple shadows linger,
    And stars look down on peace that nature brings,
A voice we love comes from the vine-clad porchway,
    We listen for each word when Mother sings.

When mother sings the songs she loved in childhood,
    She takes us with her to the old home place;
Her plaintive notes hold many a sigh and quiver,
    While tears flow down her lovely, saintly face.

When mother sings we feel a hallowed Presence,
    A soul inspiring melody that softly rings,
Of life and hope and glorious dreams of Heaven,
    We feel this vital thrill when mother sings.

The sweetest type of heaven is home.

I call to remembrance the unfeigned faith that is in thee, which dwelt first in thy grandmother Lois and thy mother Eunice . . . (2 Tim. 1:5).

B lessed is the memory of an old-fashioned mother. It floats to us like the beautiful perfume of some wood blossoms. The music of other voices may be lost, but the enchanting memory of hers will echo in our soul forever.

> When God made the stars and the sunshine
> The rain and the flowers and the trees
> He also created a mother
> Because she was like unto these. *Grace F. Trude.*

Youth fades, love droops; the leaves of friendship fall, but a mother's secret hope outlives them all.

. . . Despise not thy mother when she is old (Prov. 23:22).

I love old mothers—mothers with white hair,
And kindly eyes, and lips grown softly sweet
With murmured blessings over sleeping babes.
There is a something in their quiet grace
That speaks the calm of Sabbath afternoons;
A knowledge in their deep, unfaltering eyes,
That far outreaches all philosophy.
Time with caressing touch, about them weaves
The silver-threaded fairy-shawl of age,
While all the echoes of forgotten songs
Seem joined to lend a sweetness to their speech.
Old mothers!—as they pass, one sees again
Old garden-walks, old roses and old loves.

Charles S. Ross.

A house is built by human hands, but a home is built by human hearts.

Eye hath not seen, nor ear heard, neither have entered into the heart of man, the things that God hath prepared for them that love Him (1 Cor. 2:9).

It will not take long for God to make up to you in the next world for all you have suffered in this. As you enter Heaven, He may say: "Give this man one of those towered and colonnaded palaces on that ridge of gold overlooking the sea of glass.

"Give this woman a home among the amaranthine blooms and between those fountains tossing in the everlasting sunlight. Give her a couch canopied with rainbows to pay her for all the fatigues of wifehood and motherhood, and housekeeping, from which she had no rest for forty years.

"Give these newly-arrived souls from earth the costliest things and roll to their door the grandest chariots, and hang on their walls the sweetest harps that ever responded to singers seraphic. Give to them rapture on rapture, jubilee on jubilee, heaven on heaven. They had a hard time on earth earning a livelihood, nursing sick children, waiting on querulous old age, or were compelled to work after they got short-breathed, rheumatic and dim-sighted.

"Chamberlains of Heaven, keepers of the King's robe, banqueters of eternal royalty, make up to them a hundredfold, a thousandfold, a millionfold, for all they suffered from swaddling clothes to shroud, and let all those who, whether on the hills, or in the temples, or on the throne, or on Jasper walls, were helped and sanctified and prepared for this heavenly realm by trial and pain, stand up and wave their scepters."

And I looked and behold—nine-tenths of the ransomed rose to their feet, and nine-tenths of the scepters swayed to and fro in the light of the sun that never sets; and then I understood better than before that *trouble comes for beneficent purposes, and that on the coldest nights the aurora is brightest in the northern heavens.*

T. DeWitt Talmage.

. . . And be content with such things as ye have for he hath said, I will never leave thee nor forsake thee (Heb. 13:5).

Kingsley once had a visit from a friend who had just returned home from tiger hunting in the Himalayas. Oh, how insignificant and little he found the village where Kingsley lived. How he commiserated poor Kingsley, compelled to be continually in such a surrounding when the world was so great and vast.

Kingsley replied with a happy smile, "It is now some years ago that I realized that my dwelling place must be my prison or my palace. Thank God! He has made it a palace."

Jesus Christ was never controlled by His circumstances—He bent them to meet His needs.

. . . Though our outward man perish, yet the inward man is renewed day by day (2 Cor. 4:16).

When the ground in London was cleared of the old buildings to make the new Kingsway, it lay for a year exposed to the light and air. A strange sight drew naturalists to the ruins. In some cases the soil had not felt the touch of spring since the day when the Romans sailed up the Thames and beached upon its strand. When the sunlight poured its life upon this uncovered soil, a host of flowers sprang up. Some were unknown in England. They were plants the Romans had brought with them. Hidden away in the darkness, lying dormant under the mass of bricks and mortar, they seemed to have died, but under the new conditions, obeying the law of life, they escaped from death and blossomed into a new beauty.

So may it be with every life, however crushed and bruised by sorrow, however blighted by sin. *It needs only to be laid open to the breath of God's Spirit, the sunshine of His love, and the healing atmosphere of His grace in Christ Jesus, and a new life, with new possibilities and new beauties, will arise, however desolate at present the scene may appear.*

> Thus ever on through life we find
>   To trust, O Lord, is best,
> Who serve Thee with a quiet mind
>   Find in Thy service rest.
> Their outward troubles may not cease,
>   But this their joy will be—
> "Thou wilt keep him in perfect peace
>   Whose mind is stayed on Thee."

But we all with open face beholding as in a glass the Glory of the Lord, are changed into the same image from glory to glory even as by the Spirit of the Lord (2 Cor. 3:18).

We recall the gracious personality of the late Dr. F. B. Meyer. Of him, when he had finished his course, it was said: "He was close on eighty-two years old, and to the end worked with the fullness of energy of a man who had found the Sabbatic quiet of a ripe old age, not in idleness, but in restful fellowship with God."

His face, as the years passed, seemed to grow more beautiful, as the sorrows of the world, and the peace of God, which were both his daily possession, shaped and refined his features. *He was the stuff that prejudices men in favour of Jesus Christ his Lord.* He was evergreen.

Lovely faces mark the men who walk and talk with God.

Blessed is the man whose strength is in thee . . . (Psalm 84:5).

A blind woman once said, "I am very happy in my religion. Although I have never had sight, there are many beautiful things that God has put in the world. These I have seen."

She had never seen a star-lit sky, a rainbow, a zigzag lightning flash, the halo of mist around the crest of the mountain, a million fishes splashing in a tropical river at sunrise. She had never see a baby, a smile, a magnolia tree in bloom, a green wheat field, a wooded hillside in autumn, a thick white cloud, phoshorescence playing across the ocean breakers at night, or a rainbow painted by the setting sun across a canvas of dark clouds. Yet, she spoke of seeing many beautiful things.

She had sensed the fragrance of the rosebud. She had heard the voice of God through the greeting of friends; tasted His providence in the cool water, and felt His presence through her fingertips as she studied her Braille New Testament. The beauty of the world made her happy.

The old colored saint expressed his secret of a happy life in the words, "I have learned how to cooperate with the inevitable."

. . . This thing is from me . . . (2 Chron. 11:4—RV).

> Shut in? Ah, yes, that's so,
> As far as getting out may go,
> Shut in away from earthly cares,
> But not shut out from Him who cares.
>
> Shut in from many a futile quest,
> But Christ can be your daily Guest.
> He's not shut out by your four walls,
> But hears and answers all your calls.
>
> Shut in with God. Oh that should be
> Such a wonderful opportunity.
> Then after you have done your best,
> In God's hands safely leave the rest.

Only the master must say where and for what purpose he needs his servant most. A wise master never wastes his servant's time.

Yea, the darkness hideth not from thee; but the night shineth as the day; the darkness and the light are both alike to thee (Psalm 139:12).

A t eighty-four, Amelia Barr was at work on her sixty-sixth book. Her secret for such activity is quiet and darkness. All forms of life need them. The plant cannot bloom continuously; it must lie its time in the earth in quiet and darkness. Trees have their winter rest. All animals must sleep.

The human being cannot maintain efficient life unless it retreats daily into death, back into nothingness, cessation, stillness. When we lie down at night in sleep all the invisible workmen of the body set about their tasks, cleaning, repairing, restoring, adjusting, just as the cleaners go over a locomotive when it comes in from its run. These workers operate only in quiet and darkness.

It is the same with the mind. Keep constantly on the go and your thoughts get clogged, you have confusion, imperfect judgment, awkwardness. Most of the worries that beset us would vanish of themselves if we would take a long bath in quietness and darkness. Evil, fevered, extravagant, hurtful ideas and beliefs are by-products of too much activity; they dissolve in quiet and darkness.

Never mind whether you sleep or not, just be still. It is in quiet and darkness you hear those still, small voices your life misses in the hurly-burly. It is there you find God.

I will both lay me down in peace and sleep, for thou Lord, only makest me dwell in safety (Psalm 4:8).

When my sun of life is low,
  When the dewy shadows creep,
Say for me before I go,
  "Now I lay me down to sleep."

I am at the journey's end,
  I have sown and I must reap;
There are no more ways to mend,
  "Now I lay me down to sleep."

Nothing more to doubt or dare,
  Nothing more to give or keep;
Say for me the children's prayer,
  "Now I lay me down to sleep."

Who has learned along the way—
  Primrose path or stony steep—
More of wisdom than to say,
  "Now I lay me down to sleep?"

What have you more wise to tell
  When the shadows round me creep?
All is over, all is well . . .
  "Now I lay me down to sleep."   *Bert Leston Taylor.*

The last hours of the venerable Dr. Nott were peculiarly impressive. Visions of his childhood home floated continually before him and the name of his mother was continually upon his lips; the last words he uttered were the last words of prayer his mother taught him when a child—"Now I lay me down to sleep."

Every life needs its altar.

Thou didst encourage me with strength (Psalm 138:3—RV).

One year at the Mildmay Conference, C. H. Spurgeon said: "After a period of continued pain, with little sleep, I sat up as best I could one morning in my bed, and in an agony of pain, cried to the Lord for deliverance. I believed fully that He could deliver me there and then. I went the length of pleading that He was my Father, and I said, 'If it were my child that suffered so, I would not let him suffer any longer if I could help him. Thou canst help, and by Thy Fatherly love I plead with Thee to give me rest.'

"I felt that I could add, 'Nevertheless, not as I will, but as Thou wilt!' But I went first where Christ went first, saying, 'Father if it be possible, let this cup pass from me.' I shall never forget my success in my appeal. Within a few moments the pain subsided, and very soon I slept most peacefully."

Faith purifies the heart and transforms the life.

_____

Thou shalt lie down and none shall make thee afraid . . . (Job 11:19).

There is a wonderful portrait in the Bible of a man, an old man, a gray haired man, lying on his couch, with his head resting on his hand, looking at the face of his boy. In the last hour of his life, he looks across to a corner in the room and there stands his harp. Oh, how often he has strummed that harp, but there it stands and he has no more ability to put his hands on it and make it go. He looks to the other side of the room and there stands his staff with which, out of the brush and the briars, he had so often drawn his tender lambs, when they got into trouble. Then he looks at the face of his boy and says, "My boy, I am going away just now, but you remain perfectly safe and steadfast and sure. Stand true to God and to the highest and best." Then as he listens to Heavenly music, his lips move and he murmurs, "Yea, though I walk through the valley of the shadow of death, I will fear no evil, for thou art with me; thy rod and thy staff they comfort me." He drops back on his pillow and goes to sleep.

That is David. Under God's low bending sky, under God's stars of everlasting promise, in God's own companionship, he just went to sleep.

The Christian life is set to music; the un-Christian way is set to misery.

. . . The unsearchable riches of Christ (Eph. 3:8).

I saw a bee exploring the wealth of a nasturtium flower. Then I thought of all the flowers in my garden, and of all the flowers in my neighborhood, and of all the flowers in my country—growing in quiet meadows, on heathery moor and in twilight glen; the floral splendors of other lands—bending on the blowing plain, or nestling in the hollows of the towering heights; to the inconceivable luxuriance of the tropics.

And then I came back to my bee, and I thought of that bee as setting out to explore the floral wonders of the universe! Then I came back to the apostle, equally busy extracting juices "sweeter than honey and the honeycomb" and almost bewildered by the vast and overwhelming glories of his inheritance. *The unsearchable riches of Christ—wealth inexplorable!*

And his feet shall stand in that day upon the Mount of Olives . . . (Zech. 14:4).

> In the crimson of the morning, in the whiteness of
>   the noon,
>   In the amber glory of the day's retreat,
> In the midnight, robed in darkness, or the gleaming of
>   the moon,
>   I listen for the coming of His feet.
>
> I have heard His weary footsteps on the sands of Galilee
>   On the temple's marble pavement, on the street,
> Worn with weight of sorrow, faltering up the slopes
>   of Calvary,
>   The sorrow of the coming of His feet.
>
> Down the minster-aisles of splendor, from between
>   the cherubim,
>   Through the wondering throng, with motion strong
>   and fleet,
> Sounds His victor tread, approaching with a music far
>   and dim,
>   The music of the coming of His feet.
>
> Sandled not with sheen of silver, girdled not with
>   woven gold,
>   Weighted not with shimmering gems and odors sweet,
> But white-winged and shod with glory in the Tabor light
>   of old—
>   The glory of the coming of His feet.
>
> He is coming, oh my spirit! with His everlasting peace,
>   With His blessedness, immortal and complete;
> He is coming, oh, my spirit, and His coming brings
>   release,
>   I listen for the coming of His feet.

"Be ready in the morning . . . "(Exod. 34:2).

. . . Forgetting those things which are behind, and reaching forth unto those things which are before (Phil. 3:13).

The amazing thing in regard to our text is that it was written by a man advanced in years and nearing the end of his life. It is an inspiring vision to see men who are thus advancing in years piling fresh fuel upon their altar fires. There is something contagious about the individual who preserves a militant soul and who goes forth to slay dragons as bravely and with as much knightly buoyancy and song as in the days of earlier conflict.

Nearing the end of his days, in prison in Rome, how fares it with Paul now?

Hear him say, "Reaching forth to the things which are before, I press toward the mark for the prize of the high calling of God in Christ Jesus."

Refresh your soul with a drink from this spring!

I therefore so run, not as uncertainly; so fight I, not as one that beateth the air (1 Cor. 9:26).

> Give me the man who facing winter's blast,
> Hails coming spring;
> Sings of returning dawn
> In darkest night;
> Knows gloom must flee before
> Triumphant light;
> And still fights on,
> Though crushed and beaten down,
> Till he has won the fight
> And gained the crown.

Strong minds suffer without complaining; weak minds complain without suffering.

For what merit is there in standing a beating for doing wrong? But if you bear patiently with suffering when you are doing right, this is pleasing to God (1 Peter 2:20—Berkeley Version).

To stand with a smile upon your face, against a stake from which you cannot get away—that no doubt, is heroic.

But true glory is not resignation to the inevitable. To stand unchained with perfect liberty to go away, held only by the higher claims of duty, and let the fire creep up to the heart—this is heroism.

> Peter, outworn
> And menaced by the sword,
> Shook off the dust of Rome;
> And, as he fled,
> Met one with eager face,
> Hastening cityward,
> And, to his vast amaze,
> It was the Lord.
>
> "Lord, whither goest Thou?"
> He cried, importunate;
> And Christ replied,
> "Peter I suffer loss,
> I go to take thy place,
> To bear thy cross."
>
> Then Peter bowed his head,
> Discomforted;
> Then at the Master's feet,
> Found grace complete,
> And courage, and new faith,
> And turned, with Him
> To death.   *John Oxenham.*

Our character is determined by what we would do if every restraint were removed.

. . . Consider the lilies of the field . . . (Matt. 6:28).

Just as the flower is made to receive the sun and only reaches its individuality when filled with sunshine . . . so the human heart is made for Christ and it is incomplete until it receives Him. It is the complement of its being and it unfolds and blossoms into all its predestined powers when quickened by His life, inspired by His presence, planted and watered by His indwelling life and love.

The fifteenth chapter of John is perhaps the most perfect unfolding of this message of the abiding life. The three keynotes are "in Him," "in us," and "abide." We are not to struggle. We are not to try. We are not to do. We are not to be. We are simply to let Him be and so abide that His life shall flow through us as the sap flows through the branches of the vine, and the rich clusters hang without an effort through the spontaneous life which flows through all the beautiful organism of the plant. *A. B. Simpson.*

Life from the center is a life of unhurried peace and power. It is simple, it is amazing, it is triumphant, it is radiant. It takes not time, but it occupies all our time. Thomas Kelley.

Let your light so shine before men that they may see your good works and glorify your Father which is in Heaven (Matt. 5:16).

Halford Luccock tells us that Norman Angell once introduced a friend in this way. "This is Harold. He doesn't do anything. He just is."

We shall be remembered more for what we are than for anything we do. Deeds are always the product of our nature, and accurately reflect what is in us. When we are judged by our deeds, it will be because the deeds wrongly done reveal the lack of Christian content in ourselves and not because of the deeds themselves. In a very real sense what we do is an indication of what we are.

A Christian never is—he is becoming.

. . . Be of good cheer; it is I; be not afraid (Matt. 14:27).

When all the haunting shadows of the night
Come thronging round me with a sudden sweep,
Whispering and echoing the fears I keep
By faith and hope and prayer, hidden from sight;

When white-lipped doubt suggests that my delight
Is a delusion, and my faith a leap
Into the dark, and that the years will reap
In pain and trouble what has seemed so right:

And when the floods encompass me about,
And the sweet vision of my Lord doth fade
In the blind darkness, and the words He said
Seem lost; I feel once more His hand stretched out;

Once more He speaks, "Tis I, be not afraid;
O thou of little faith, why didst thou doubt?"

Lucy Guiness Kumm.

Our doubts are traitors and make us lose the good we fight to win.

The Lord taketh pleasure in his people; he will beautify the meek with salvation (Psalm 149:4).

"A re you cold this morning?" said a city man on a dull day to a newspaper boy.

"I was, sir, before I met you," answered the little poet of the pavement.

Phillips Brooks was the soul of saintliness—saintliness with red blood. To see him walk along a Boston street made the day, if it was dark and gloomy, bright and sunny. A man once found refuge from a sudden storm in a doorway in Boston. Afterwards he said, "The day was brighter because of the man who shared the doorway with me." It was Phillips Brooks who had shared the doorway with him that day. No deed was done. Brooks just *was* Christian and that was enough to let light shine through him into another life.

The atmosphere of a whole church has been changed by a single beautiful life within that church; the tone of an entire schoolroom has been made different by the spirit of a noble Christian youth who studied there.

The influence of a person whose heart God has touched is like a breath of fresh air in a hot room. Some Christians I have known were sweeter than the breath of roses in radiant June.

Robert Louis Stevenson once said, "Worth-while folks don't just happen."

. . . Clothe yourselves with tenderness of heart, kindliness, humble-mindedness, gentleness, patient endurance (Col. 3:12—Berkeley Version).

R ev. Robert Newton, the Wesleyan pulpit orator, and his bride began their married life by retiring twice each day to pray with and for each other. This practice they kept up, when opportunity served, to the end of life. When an old man, Mr. Newton remarked, "In the course of a short time, my wife and I shall celebrate the jubilee of our marriage; and I know not, that during the fifty years of our union, an unkind look or an unkind word has ever passed between us."

> My Uncle Job one summer's day
>   Laid aside his numerous woes,
> And from the hedge beside the way
>   Plucked Aunt Jane a crimson rose.
>
> And skylarks carolled to the sun,
>   And fairies danced the road along
> Singing, singing, "Oh, well done!"
>   And Uncle's heart became a song!

I never hear a gentle, loving word, but my heart thrills and softens under it, and I involuntarily thank our Heavenly Father that He has put such a blessed keynote in the voice of humanity.

A cup brimful of sweet water cannot spill even one drop of bitter water however suddenly jolted.

I tell you that, if these should hold their peace, the stones would immediately cry out (Luke 19:40).

Tell the birds amidst the buds of spring not to sing; tell the waters welling from the depths not to flow; tell the happy child not to laugh and jump; tell the sun and stars not to shine; and when these have obeyed you, then tell the soul which has been baptized with the love of God that it must not speak of him, and it will laugh you to scorn. It cannot but speak what it has seen and heard. *F. B. Meyer.*

Religion as a dull habit is not that for which Christ lived and died.

Let brotherly love continue (Hebrews 13:1).

There is a beautiful legend regarding sharing one another's burdens. Two brothers had adjoining fields. On the evening after the grain had been cut and shocked, the elder brother said to his wife: "My younger brother is unable to bear the burden and heat of the day. I will arise, take of my shocks, and place them with his, without his knowledge." The younger brother, being actuated by the same benevolent motives, said within himself, "My elder brother has a family, and I have none. I will arise, take of my shocks and place them with his."

Judge their mutual astonishment when, on the following day, they found their respective shocks undiminished. This transpired for several nights, when each resolved in his own mind to stand guard and solve the mystery. They did so; and on the following night they met each other halfway between their respective shocks with their arms full. On the spot where they met, ground hallowed by such brotherly love and care, tradition says the Temple was built.   *Vivian Ahrendt.*

God's grace toward us should make us gracious toward others.

. . . It doth not yet appear what we shall be: but we know that, when he shall appear, we shall be like him . . . (1 John 3:2).

In the mountain forests to the west of Dohnavur (India) our children find the cocoon of the atlas moth. It hangs from a twig, like a small brown bag tied up, left there and forgotten—a mere two inches of papery bag. And however often we see it, we are never prepared for the miracle that emerges. For miracle it is: a large, almost birdlike creature, struggles through the very narrow neck of the bag. It has wings of crimson and pink and blended green of various soft tones, shading off into terra-cotta, brown, old-gold. Each wing has a window made of a clear substance like a delicate flake of talc, and on the edge of each is a pattern of wavy lines or dots, or some other dainty device. From wing-tip to wing-tip, nine, sometimes ten inches of beauty, one of God's lovely wonders—that is what comes out of the brown paper bag. Nothing preserved in a glass case can show it, for the colors fade; but fresh from the hands of the Creator, it is like something seen in a dream.

What if our life within these detaining months or years be like the life within the dull brown bag of the cocoon? One day something will emerge to the glory of His grace. Can we not, then, sustained by the Bread of heaven and the good Wine, continue in this hidden labor and spiritual fight till the sunset colors kindle and the stars appear?   *Amy Carmichael.*

The fullest and most complete life comes out of the most completely empty life.

Now unto Him that is able to do exceeding abundantly above all that we ask or think . . . (Eph. 3:20).

> God—Thou hast made the world so beautiful!
> A flock of birds on pinions fleet and strong,
> Then—though it were not yet enough to soar—
>   Gave to them song.
> God—Thou hast made the world so beautiful;
> A bower of June with roses gay abloom,
> Then—though it were not yet enough to grow—
>   Gave them perfume.
> God—Thou hast made the world so beautiful;
> A million beings, soul their priceless gem,
> Then—though it were not yet enough to live—
>   Gave love to them.   *Theodosia Pearce.*

All the wealth brought to earth from heaven above is yours as the gift of Christ's love.

Come ye yourselves apart . . . (Mark 6:31).

In speaking to a group of friends about his work habits, George Washington Carver said: "First I go into the woods and gather specimens and listen to the things God has to say to me. After I have had my morning talk with God, I go to my laboratory and begin to carry out His wishes for the day. If I fail, it is my failure; and if I succeed, God's will has been done."

We remember, Father, that our Master rose up very early to commune with Thee. Remind us to begin each day with prayer.

Ten minutes spent in Christ's society every day—aye, two minutes—will make the whole day different.   *Henry Drummond.*

Let us put by some hour of every day for holy things.
                                               Clinton Scollard.

Whereby are given unto us exceeding great and precious promises . . .
(2 Peter 1:4).

Promises cover the whole period of human life . . . You cannot
bring yourselves unto a condition for which you cannot find
in God's Word some promise. Therefore, there are promises of
God to the ignorant; to the poor; to the neglected; to the
burdened; to the oppressed; to the discouraged; to the solitary; to
the imprisoned; to the sick; to the heart-broken; to the remorseful;
to the weak; to the strong; to the timid; to the brave; to every
affliction; to every one of its exigencies; to every sphere of duty; to
all perils; to every temptation that waylays good men in their
journey.

There are promises for joy; for sorrow; for victory; for defeat; for
adversity; for prosperity; for those who run; for those who walk;
for those who can only stand still. Old age has its garlands as full
and fragrant as youth. The sick, the dying—all men, everywhere
and always, have their promises of God.

> And should my soul be torn with grief
>   Upon my shelf I find
> A little volume, torn and thumbed,
>   For comfort just designed.
> I take my little Bible down
>   And read its pages o'er,
> And when I part from it I find
>   I'm stronger than before.

Edgar A. Guest.

I will therefore that men pray everywhere, lifting up holy hands, without wrath and doubting (1 Tim. 2:8).

Y ou can pray for any need—for lengthened life, as Hezekiah did; for help, as Daniel did; for mercy, as David did; for rain, as Elijah did; for a son, as Hannah did; for grace, as Paul did. You can pray, too, anywhere—in the deep, like Jonah; on the sea or housetop, like Peter; on your bed, like Hezekiah; in the mountain, like Jesus; in the wilderness, like Hagar; in the street, like Jairus; in a cave, like David; on the cross, like the dying thief.

You can pray, too, anyhow—short, as Peter and the Publican did; long, like Moses at the consecration of the Tabernacle, or Solomon at the dedication of the temple. You can pray in your secret thoughts, as Nehemiah did before Darius; or aloud, as did the Syro-Phoenician woman; in tears, as Magdalene did; in groans or songs, as David did.

You can pray anytime—in the morning, as David did; at noon, as Daniel did; at midnight, as Silas did; in childhood, as Samuel did; in youth, as Timothy did; in manhood as the centurion did; in age, as Simeon did; in sickness, as Job did; or in death, as did Jacob and the dying Christ.

Robert G. Lee.

Careless prayer is presumption; commanded prayer is obedience.

Thou shalt abide for me many days . . . so will I also be for thee (Hosea 3:3).

Whether the paths of life be draped with flowers or strewn with cypresses, His voice of unchanging and unchangeable faithfulness rings its echo, "Lo, I am with you always, even to the close of days."

Having God with us, life shall bloom like the spring fields, have perfume like the spring flowers and have radiance like the fields in June.

> Of all the prizes,
> That earth can give,
>   This is the best:
> To find Thee, Lord,
> A living Presence near
>   And in Thee rest!
>
> Friends, fortune, fame,
> Or what might come to me—
>   I count all loss
> If I find not
> Companionship
>   With Thee!

Because he hath inclined his ear unto me, therefore will I call upon him as long as I live (Psalm 116:2).

I can take my telescope and look millions of miles into space; but I can go away to my room and in prayer get nearer to God and Heaven than I can when assisted by all the telescopes of earth. *Sir Isaac Newton.*

The mother of Madame Chiang Kai-shek had the custom of retiring to the third floor of her home to a room she kept for the purpose of tarrying long for God's daily instructions. When sought for advice, her answer would be, "You must wait until tomorrow so that I can ask my Master all about it and get His guidance." Asking God was not a matter of spending five minutes asking God to bless her children and grant her requests. It meant waiting upon God until she felt His leading.

Keep your tryst with God in star-glow and noonday heat.

Or what man is there of you whom if his son ask bread, will he give him a stone? Or if he ask a fish, will he give him a serpent? If ye then, being evil, know how to give good gifts unto your children, how much more shall your Father which is in heaven give good things to them that ask him? (Matt. 7:9-11).

As you walk in obedience to the Lord and in loving fellowship with Him, as you allow His Word to dwell in you richly, you will discover that God has a special prayer promise for you. It is His gracious gift to you because He can trust you to pray aright. He says to you, "You may ask what you will, and it shall be done unto you."

He gives you this liberty to ask whatever you will because through your growth in Christ, you have reached a position of intelligent responsibility in His Kingdom. He recognizes you and honors you as a son, who has attained wisdom and understanding to ask aright for His interests and His glory.

Prayer is not overcoming God's reluctance, but laying hold of His highest willingness.

. . . For the former things are passed away (Rev. 21:4).

> Some day of days, some dawning yet to be,
>   I shall be clothed with immortality;
> And in that day I shall not greatly care,
>   That Jane spilt candle-grease upon the stair.
> It will not vex me then, as once it did,
>   That careless hands have chipped my teapot lid;
> So for that day I lay me at Thy feet,
>   Then keep me sweet, my Savior, keep me sweet.
>   *Fay Inchfawn.*

Could the weary pilgrim stand at heaven's gate and view the world behind him, not a thought of all the past would disturb him now.

God is our refuge and strength, a very present help in trouble (Psalm 46:1).

Many people are simply trying, but not trusting, and there is no more help in that than in the faint efforts of the poor little kitten which had fallen into a well, and was in the process of being rescued. The farmer had heard its pitiful cries and noticed that it had climbed out of the water and was hanging onto a ledge in the brick work. He gently dropped a bucket down beneath in and tried to induce it to drop in, but the kitten simply reached out its little paws and then drew them back timorously, and cried and cried again in its helplessness and despair. This was all in vain. The kitten could not be rescued until it would let go the ledge and commit itself to the bucket. The struggle lasted a long while until at last, tired and ready to fall, it ventured; there was a little plunge, and the farmer knew by the added weight that the refugee was safely caught and it was a small matter now to land his burden on solid ground.

Exactly so we hesitate and struggle until at last, tired, we just let go and then it is easy for God to do anything for us. The prayer of faith is a transaction which we must settle at a definite moment, and ever after count it settled.

Our helplessness brings His help. Nothing is required of us but poverty of spirit (poor in spirit). We do not even have to know how to cry. The more helpless we seem to be, the easier it is to receive.

My presence shall go with Thee . . . (Exod. 33:14).

All the time I was climbing alone, I had the strong feeling that I was accompanied by a second person. This feeling was so strong that it completely eliminated all loneliness I might otherwise have felt.

It even seemed that I was tied to my 'companion' by a rope, and that if I slipped 'he' would hold me. I remember constantly glancing over my shoulder, and once, when after reaching the highest point, I stopped to try to eat some mint cake, I carefully divided it and turned round with one half in my hand. It was almost a shock to find no one to whom to give it.

It seemed to me that this presence was a strong, helpful and friendly one, and it was not until Camp VI was sighted that the link connecting me, as it seemed at the time, to the beyond, was snapped, and although Shipton and the camp were but a few yards away, I suddenly felt alone." *Experience of F. S. Smythe in his lone attempt to climb Mount Everest.*

In Christ I am alive. Cut off from Him, I am a withered branch.

My meditation of Him shall be sweet . . . (Psalm 104:34).

I heard a Quaker lady, who had to spend half an hour every day sitting quietly and doing nothing, calling it her still lesson. I wish we could enjoy such a half-hour daily in God's presence. Our still lesson would be one of the most useful lessons of the day.

Let us seek to become better acquainted with God by more inward and diligent meditation over the Word and on Himself.

How rare it is to find a soul quiet enough to hear God speak.

. . . The morning stars sang together and all the Sons of God shouted for joy (Job 38:7).

An author has visualized a radio announcer of the Universe depicting a scene like this:

"It is the dawn of God's eternal day. I hear the Universal announcer give the universal ring: It goes ringing—ringing—ringing to the uttermost galaxy of stars so that every creature hears.

"The announcer says, 'We will now begin the opening program for God's New Day. The first number to be sung will be by the angels of the Universe. They have decided to sing the song they sang to the shepherds on the hillsides of Galilee two thousand years ago':

" 'Glory to God in the highest—on earth peace—good will toward men!'

"We can hear those voices ringing—ringing—ringing throughout the Universe.

"The announcer then states that the next number will be Coronation by every voice in the Universe.

"I hear Isaiah with millions of the blessed singers of Israel lead off from yonder galaxy of stars.

"I hear David and his mighty harp orchestra coming in with millions of harps from another galaxy of stars from another direction joining in singing that great hymn.

"I hear Beethoven, with millions and millions of his orchestral instruments coming in from another galaxy of stars from another direction.

"I hear also, a mighty choir of colored people, who sing as no peoples have ever sung, coming in from another galaxy of stars.

"I hear Ira D. Sankey with his choir of millions and millions of gospel singers coming in from another galaxy of stars.

"Accompanying I hear God's infinite organ lifting the whole into such a symphony of music as will make the universal arches ring.

"I hear them singing: 'All hail the power of Jesus' name.'

"This mighty concert perfectly reverberating by radio throughout the entire universe annihilates time and distance."

I will never, never let go thy hand (Isa. 41:13—Modern Trans.).

> I promise thee
> That I, to whom the pillars of the earth belong,
> Will bear thee up and keep thy spirit strong.
>
> I promise thee
> That none shall add a furlong to the mile
> That thou must walk, through this long little while.
>
> I promise thee
> Thy private shadow shall not shadow ever
> The path of thy beloved fellow-lover.
>
> I promise thee that though it tarry, yet the day will come
> When I shall call thee Home.   *Amy Carmichael.*

Life holds nothing within it which Christ has not conquered.

. . . The fruit of the Spirit is love, joy, peace, longsuffering, gentleness, goodness, faith, meekness, temperance . . . (Gal. 5:22, 23).

There is a little fable of an angel and a rosebud. The angel who cares for the flowers slumbered one spring day in the shade of a rosebud. Awaking he said, "Most beautiful of my children, I thank you for your refreshing odor and cool shade. Could you ask now any favor, how willingly would I grant it."

"Adorn me then, with a new charm!" replied the rosebud. So the angel adorned the loveliest of flowers with simple moss. Sweetly it stood there, a lovely moss rose, the most beautiful of all roses.

Close beside everyone stands One greater than an angel, who holds in His hands all gifts and graces. He looks into your face as you pray for more grace and asks what new adornment He shall give you.

As the flower in reaching toward the sun reaches its own full life, so in reaching toward Christ, you reach your own fullest life.

If . . . God command thee . . . thou shalt be able . . . (Exod. 18:23).

However much the heart may ache with loneliness
Or fraught with fear the path we take
   In deep distress,
   We must go on.

Never to faint amid the heat of noonday sun,
Nor wail because of bleeding feet;
   The race begun,
   We must go on.

Up—up the rugged stone-ribbed slope of suffering,
Hands to the plow, hearts strong with hope,
   Whatever the day may bring,
   We must go on.
                        Sybil Leonard Armes

God will not allow anything to come to me that He and I together can't handle.

Ah Lord God! behold, thou hast made the heaven and the earth by thy great power and stretched out arm, and there is nothing too hard for thee (Jer. 32:17).

I f God in Christ can paint the blush on the bud which hangs from the limb of the rose, and make the dewdrops of morning tremble like molten diamonds on the virgin-white lip of the lily; if He can plant the rivers in lines of rippling silver, and can cover His valley floors with carpets of softest green, tacked down with lovely daisies and laughing daffodils; if He can scoop out the basin of the seven seas and pile up the great granite of the mountains until they pierce the turquoise skies; if He can send a Niagara thundering on a mighty and majestic ministrelsy from century to century; if He can fuel and refuel the red-throated furnace of a million suns to blaze His universe with light; if on the lovely looms of heaven, He can weave the delicate tapestry of a rainbow, and at eventide fashion a fleece of crimson to curtain the couch of the dying sun, and across the black bosom of the night that follows bind a glittering girdle spangled with ten thousand stellar jewels: then I do not doubt His power to save and keep us and to ultimately give us an order of life in which righteousness "shall cover the earth as the waters cover the sea."

The power that raised Jesus Christ from the dead will work within me today to the degree that I permit it.

. . . I will trust and not be afraid . . . (Isa. 12:2).

I distinctly remember, while quite a lad, being in my uncle's house one night during a tremendous tempest. The older folks were all afraid; but I had really trusted myself with the Lord Jesus and I did not dare to fear. The baby was upstairs, and nobody was brave enough to fetch it down, because of a big window on the stairs. I went up to the bedroom and brought the child to its mother; and then read a Psalm and prayed with my relatives, who were trembling in terror. There was real danger, for a haystack was set on fire a short distance away, but I was as calm as in the sunshine of a summer's day, not because I was naturally courageous, but because I had unshaken confidence in my Lord.

This was told by C. H. Spurgeon in later life, when the praying lad had become the praying preacher, and had gathered together a great church of praying people.

If I tremble, let me tremble bravely.

. . . The Lord blessed the latter end of Job more than the beginning . . .
(Job 42:12).

Thou, Lord, canst transform my thorn into a flower. I want my thorn transformed into a flower.

Job got the sunshine after the rain, but had the rain all been waste? Job wants to know, I want to know, if the shower had nothing to do with the shining. And Thou canst tell me. Thy Cross canst tell me. Thou hast crowned Thy sorrow. Be this my crown, O Lord. I only triumph in Thee when I have learned the radiance of the rain. *George Matheson.*

Sorrow comes to stretch out places in our hearts for joy.

_____

. . . The clouds also dropped water (Judg. 5:4).

H ave you ever wondered how the sea birds get their drinking water? Sometimes they sail thousands of miles from shore. What are their springs amid those wastes of tossing brine?

Not below, but above: in the clouds!

When a storm comes up, if you are on shipboard you may see the birds winging toward it from all directions. They have scented it from afar with their wonderful bird organs, and they haste to their descending springs. They wheel under the drops gleefully and gulp the water down in glad mouthfuls. Thus they find fresh water in mid ocean.

Brothers and sisters featherless, when next you find yourselves in the desert places of life, when you can see nothing but liquid salt even to the encircling horizon, when your parched tongues and your aching souls cry out for the water of life, seek not beneath you for the well springs of happiness, but look above! There in God's blue they gather, the soft caravans of bounty. *Dark on the underside, you know that the heavenward portion is all aglow with God's smile.* Rest on the waves, and turn your faces to the sky. The windows of heaven will open, and God will pour you out a blessing, that there shall not be room to receive it.   *Amos R. Wells*

I drew them with cords . . . of love . . . (Hosea 11:4).

He stood aside from his playmates,
  His sightless eyes to the sky,
And the cord in his hands was tightly drawn
  By the kite that flew so high.
In his big eyes, wondering, beautiful,
  On his pale little slender face,
There shone such a rapture, such keen delight,
  That someway it seemed out of place.
And I could no forbear to pause and ask,
  "My laddie, what pleases you so,
As you hold your kite in the far-off sky,
  Since its motion you cannot know?"

He turned and smiled as he softly said,
  And his voice with joy was full,
"I can't just explain, but it makes me glad,
  When I feel that upward pull."

That Upward Pull; it comes to us
  In the weariness of strife.
When we stand bewildered, blinded and hurt,
  Mid the fall of our cherished dream.
It is good to know that we cannot fail,
  If we follow the heavenly gleam.
And never an hour may be so sad,
  Nor ever a sky so dull
But we may, if we will, reach out and find
  That God-given, Upward Pull.   *Helen M. Wilson*

All our crises are finger posts pointing us upward to the cross.

. . . If any man thirst let him come unto me and drink. He that believeth on me, as the scripture hath said, From within shall flow rivers of living waters (John 7:37, 38).

Thus was the heart thrilling, soul cheering promise of the Opener of Eternal Fountains. O thirsty soul come unto me and drink. You may try everything else and your thirst will be unslaked. Left alone, you are a human desert—dry, unfertile, flowerless, songless; but you may be a garden of the Lord through which silver waters flow, wherein Heavenly songsters sing, and green fragrant things flourish through all seasons and all weathers.

The secret depths of your consciousness shall be as fresh as the streams of an invisible spring. But that is not all. Freshened and vitalized in the hidden mysteries of your own being, you shall become as the head-waters of benediction to others. Your inner brook shall break into glowing rivers and your glowing rivers shall widen into seas of living water.

I shall not use the Lord; I shall allow Him to use me.

I have loved you, saith the Lord . . . (Mal. 1:2).

> Whom the Lord loveth He chasteneth often.
> What a comforting thought, all hardness to soften!
> Quiet it brings to a questioning heart.
> "Why was it this cruel thing did befall?"
> Quickly God answers, "I love you," that's all.
> "All things must work for the good of God's lovers."
> Like a tree's leafy shade, this Bible word covers
> Hearts hot with grieving and ready to break.
> "Why is it grief made this unwelcome call?"
> Softly God answers, "I love you," that's all.
> "Whom the Lord loveth His scourging correcteth."
> As rain coming down on scorched grass, so affecteth
> This saying the soul that God's furnace has seared.
> "Why came on me all these woes that appall?"
> Kindly God answers, "I love you." That's all.

We suffer, yet do not allow the mission of suffering to be accomplished in us. May the Lord help us not to fall into that torpid state in which our crosses do us no good.

The steps of a good man are ordered by the Lord . . . (Psalm 37:23).

We have the fullest assurance that our God can and does guide His children in all things. He can signify His mind to us as to this or that particular act or movement. If not, where are we? How are we to get on? How are we to regulate our movements? Are we to be drifted hither and thither by the tide of circumstances? Are we left to blind chance, or to the mere impulse of our own will?

Thank God, it is not so. He can, in His own perfect way, give us the certainty of His mind in any given case; and, without that certainty, we should never move. Our Lord Jesus Christ can intimate his mind to his servant as to where He would have him go, and what He would have him do, and no true servant will ever think of moving or acting without such intimation. If we are not sure, let us be quiet and wait. Very often we harass and fret ourselves about movements that God would not have made us make at all.

A person once said to a friend, "I am quite at a loss to know which way to turn." "Then don't turn at all," was the friend's wise reply.

The Lord hath given me the tongue of the learned, that I should know how to speak a word in season to him that is weary: he wakeneth morning by morning, he wakeneth mine ear to hear as the learned (Isa. 50:4).

Is there ever any ground to be cast down? There are two reasons, but only two—if we are as yet unconverted, we have ground to be cast down; or if we are converted and live in sin, then we are rightly cast down. But except for these two things, there is no ground to be cast down, for all else may be brought before God in prayer with supplication and thanksgiving, and regarding all our difficulties, all our trials, we may exercise faith in the power of God, in the love of God, and in His own time help will come.

There is never a time when we may not hope in God. Whatever our necessities, however great our difficulties, and though to all appearances, help is impossible, yet, our business is to hope in God. God is not confined to this thing or that thing, or to twenty things; in ten thousand different ways, and at ten thousand different times, God may help us.

Our business is to spread our case before the Lord, in childlike simplicity to pour out all our heart before God. When we are weary and tired, either through difficulty, sore temptation, losses, crosses, or greatly reduced through sickness, under such circumstances we may turn to the Lord Jesus and remind Him of His precious promises.   *George Mueller.*

Gethsemanes are gateways.

I have remembered thy name, O Lord, in the night . . . (Psalm 119:55).

Help us now to leave our worries outside these walls! Help us to go to sleep like closing flowers at night.

> Ere thou sleepest, gently lay
> Every troubled though away;
> Put away worry and distress
> As thou puttest off thy dress.
> Drop thy burden and thy care
> In the quiet arms of prayer.
> Lord thou knowest how I live;
> All I've done amiss forgive,
> All the good I've tried to do
> Strengthen, bless and carry through,
> All I love in safety keep
> While in Thee I fall asleep.

Worry is like a rocking chair; it will give you something to do, but it will not get you anywhere.

Express your joy in singing among yourselves psalms and hymns and spiritual songs, making music in your hearts for the ears of God! (Eph. 5:18, 19—Phillips' Trans.).

"What are you doing there, Sam, strumming on the banjo and singing away all to yourself?" asked a passer-by of a happy colored man.

"Oh, I was just serenadin' mah own soul," was the quick reply.

Paul suggested that we serenade our souls by making melody in our hearts to the Lord. The Psalmist refreshed his soul with praise and said, "His praise shall continually be in my mouth."

"Her work is in the valley, but her heart is with the stars," said a homemaker of a woman who had been hired to help with domestic duties. She sang as she did her work, because, she explained, "We should do our everyday work for God."

Turn Thou, O Lord, our seculars into sacreds.

. . . He that believeth shall not make haste (Isa. 28:16).

On evenin's when the southern breeze comes soft an' sweet an' mild, just clingin' and caressin' like the fingers of a child, it brings a kind of longin' to a feller's heart to be at peace, an' feelin' full of love t'wards all humanity; it thaws out all the hardness an' the spite he's stored away an' charged 'gainst some that's wronged him, to be used some other day; it makes him mild an' yieldin' so he hardly could refuse a favor to most anyone ev'n if he knows he'll lose.

The birds an' beasts are matin', an' the trees an' growin' things are spread with all the soft new life an' beauty summer brings. It all acts like a tonic—lightens up a feller's heart; it brightens up old friendships an' helps new ones get a start; it helps a feller see the works of his Creator's hand; he gets a glimpse of mightiness that men can't understand—that is, if he's a farmer, with a real farmer's heart—when the mild, sweet southern breezes of the early summer start. *Ernest A. Wendt.*

Recently I asked a Georgia friend why Southerners were always so slow and deliberate. "I asked my great grandfather that same question once," he replied, "and I'll never forget his answer: *'Son, it just doesn't pay to be in a hurry. You always pass up much more than you catch up with.'"*

. . . Their strength is to sit still (Isa. 30:7).

> Be still my heart! We murmur, you and I,
> We fret and fret, while precious hours fly,
> Be still—the silent are truly blest;
> There is no rapture for a heart distressed.
>
> Be still my heart! the deep, dark night is still,
> The trees in prayer, the star above the hill.
> Be still—and to this promise softly cling,
> The silent hear the great archangels sing.
>
> *Roscoe Gilmore Scott.*

Quiet minds cannot be perplexed or frightened, but go on in fortune or misfortune at their own private pace, like a clock during a thunderstorm. *Robert Louis Stevenson.*

> Let thy soul walk softly in thee
>   Like a saint in heaven unshod
> For to be alone with silence,
>   Is to be at home with God.

The righteous shall flourish like the palm tree: he shall grow like a cedar in Lebanon (Psalm 92:12).

These trees are not trained and pruned by man: palms and cedars are trees of the Lord, and it is by His care that they flourish; even so it is with the saints of the Lord; they are His own care! These trees are evergreen and are beautiful objects at all seasons of the year. Believers are not sometimes holy and sometimes ungodly; they stand in the beauty of the Lord under all weathers. Everywhere these trees are noteworthy: no one can gaze upon a landscape in which there are either palms or cedars without his attention being fixed upon these royal growths. The followers of Jesus are the observed of all observers: like a city set on a hill, they cannot be hid.

The child of God flourishes like a palm tree, which pushes all its strength upward in one erect column without a single branch. It is a pillar with a glorious capital. It has no growth to the right nor to the left, but sends all its force heavenward, and bears its fruit as near the sky as possible. Lord, fulfill this type in me!

The cedar braves all storms, and grows near the eternal snows, the Lord Himself filling it with a sap which keeps its heart warm and its boughs strong. Lord, so let it be with me, I pray!

Charles H. Spurgeon.

. . . How much more shall your heavenly Father give the Holy Spirit to them that ask him? (Luke 11:13).

A Christian man came to me and said—expecting encouragement and approval—"I have been seeking that blessing for over thirty years."

"Brother, it's nearly time you got it then!" was the swift rejoinder.

For all these years that man was crying, "Give, give, give!" God was saying, "Receive, receive! for I do give!" If I heard my little girl crying for a piece of bread, would I tell her to cry on for another hour and then I might attend to her wants?

But what if she would not take the bread I offered, but still went on with her crying. "You silly child!" you would say.

Oh, how many silly children has the Father in His family, crying year in and year out, "Give, give!" and the Father is all the while saying, "Take, take, my child!" Let some of us give over our crying and set to work receiving! *Begin to believe God definitely for the thing you are asking of Him.*　　　　　*Rev. John McNeil.*

. . . Who hath despised the day of small things? (Zech. 4:10).

A happy life is not built up of tours abroad and pleasant holidays, but of the little clumps of violets noticed by the roadside, hidden away almost so that only those can see them who have God's peace and love in their hearts; in one long continuous chain of little joys; little whispers from the spiritual world; little gleams of sunshine on our daily work. So long have I stuck to nature and the New Testament I have only got happier and happier every day. *Edward Wilson.*

> God of the wayside weed
> Grant I may serve the humblest need.

Life is not as the sunflower, wholly in the sun, but as the violet, partly in shade, partly in sun. *There are midnights, just as there are noons, but every midnight is on the road to noon.*

> A little love, a little trust
> A soft impulse, a sudden dream,
> And life as dry as desert dust
> Is fresher than a mountain stream.

Thou surpriseth him (Psalm 21:3—Way's Trans.).

> Honey, jes' lissen: don't cry and fret,
> Dere's all day tomorrer that ain't been touched yet.
> Mought be a sunrise mek yo' heart shout,
> Look jes like Hebben turned inside out;
> Mought be awalkin' 'long on the road
> Fin' a gold nugget big as a toad.
> Mought turn a corner most any place
> Bes' friend a smilin' right in yo face.
> Heart o' mine, lissen: Why will yo fret?
> Dere's a whole day tomorrer—that ain't been touched yet!
> *Poem last recited by Bessie L. Cowie—at ninety years of age.*

You can't change the past, but you can ruin a perfectly good present by worrying about the future.

For we are laborers together with God; ye are God's husbandry, ye are God's building (1 Cor. 3:9).

One day in Edinburgh, as the new minister was making his initial calls, he called at the cobbler's shop. He talked loftily to the cobbler, as we preachers are wont to do when certain fits of stupidity possess us! When the cobbler answered back, the preacher in astonishment said, "Man, you should not be cobbling shoes, you, a man with such thoughts and such a manner of expressing those thoughts! You should not be doing secular work."

The cobbler said, "Sir, take that back!"

"What?"

"I am not doing secular work. Do you see that pair of shoes there?"

"I do."

"They belong to Widow Smith's son. Her husband died in the summer. She nearly died too, but she was kept alive by her boy. Now her boy has a paper route to help the widow keep the roof over their heads, and the bad weather is coming on; and God Almighty said to me, 'Will you cobble Widow Smith's boy's shoes so that he won't catch pneumonia and die this winter?' And I said, 'I will!' Now you preach your sermons under God Almighty's direction, as I trust you may; and I will cobble Widow Smith's boy's shoes under God Almighty's direction; and in the day when the rewards are given out, He will say to you and to me the same sentence, 'Well done, good and faithful servant.' "

Walter Binwell Hinson.

There are strange ways of serving God;
You sweep a room or turn a sod,
And suddenly to your surpise,
You hear the whir of seraphim,
And find you're under God's own eyes,
And building palaces for Him.   *Herman Hagedorn.*

Where there is no vision, the people perish . . . (Prov. 29:18).

When the modern man would be putting on his slippers, in retirement to sleep himself to death, Abraham put on his seven-league sandals and strode away from Ur of the Chaldees to Canaan; at eighty, Moses (with Aaron at eighty-three) defied Pharaoh and delivered Israel so that they were redeemed from bondage; Joshua at eighty-five concluded his military conquest; and at seventy, Paul pressed toward the mark so that in his majestic swan song he could sing, "I have fought . . . finished . . . kept," and then add with rejoicing, "henceforth there is laid up."

I have all that is stored up for me around their personalities and performances to inspire and enrich my endeavor. Is that dwelling on the past? Then let me dream of the future as the saintly seer of Patmos who saw over a stretch of two centuries the Holy City— the new land and life.

The only way to remain young is to grow old gracefully. Each age has something beautiful in it. Don't fight the fact that you are getting old—use it.

There was an enlarging and a winding about still upward . . . (Ezek. 41:7).

Why speak of those whom age is crowning,
    As going slowly down hill,
When on the heights above them shining
    Stands One who beckons upwards still?

No sad descent to death and darkness
    Is life when lived with love as guide;
But ever climbing toward the hilltop,
    Each summit gained brings visions wide.

'Tis always up the Pilgrims travel;
    While love rejoices at their side,
To feel the press of faith more strongly,
    To know He's near, whate'er betide.

As love the pilgrims forward leadeth,
    Footsteps may falter, eyes grow dim,
But ev'ry sigh He quickly heareth,
    And not a pain is hid from Him.

The steepest crags lie all behind them;
    By gentle slopes He guides the way;
Then one last step—still up—He bears them,
    To find the joy of perfect day.   *M. H.*

Gracious Father, help me to grow old gracefully, beautifully and creatively; to come to maturity majestically. Let me so fill my mind and soul with Thee that spiritual beauty may be my achievement through constant companionship with Thee. Amen.

I am in a strait betwixt two, having a desire to depart and to be with Christ; which is far better (Phil. 1:23).

When Victor Hugo was past eighty years of age, he gave expression to his religious faith in these sublime sentences: "I feel in myself the future life. I am like a forest which has been more than once cut down. The new shoots are livelier than ever. I am rising toward the sky. The sunshine is on my head. The earth gives me its generous sap, but Heaven lights me with its unknown worlds.

"You say the soul is nothing but the resultant of the bodily powers. Why then is my soul more luminous when my bodily powers begin to fail? Winter is on my head, but eternal spring is in my heart. I breathe at this hour the fragrance of the lilacs, the violets and the roses as at twenty years. The nearer I approach the end, the plainer I hear around me the immortal symphonies of the worlds which invite me. It is marvelous, yet simple."

Our hearts pant for that illustrious sunrise.

As thy days, so shall thy restfulness be (Deut. 33:25—Modern Trans.).

A little clock which had just been finished by the maker was put on a shelf in his wareroom between two older clocks who were busy ticking away the noisy seconds.

"Well," said one of the clocks to the newcomer. "So, you've started on this task. I am sorry for you; you're ticking bravely now, but you'll be tired enough before you get through thirty-three million ticks."

"Thirty-three million ticks!" said the frightened clock. "Why I never could do that!" And it stood still instantly with despair.

"Why, you silly things," said the other clock at this moment. "Why do you listen to such words? It's nothing of the kind. You've only got to make one tick this moment. There now, isn't that easy? And now another and that is just as easy, and so right along."

"Oh, if that's all," cried the new clock, "that's easily done, so here I go." And it started bravely on again, making a tick a moment and not counting the months and the millions. But at the year's end, it had made thirty-three million vibrations without knowing it.

Oh, if Christians would only live by the moment, not the year! "Day by day" is the limit of the Lord's prayer. "Sufficient unto the day is the evil thereof," said the Lord. And "as thy days, so shall thy strength be" is the promise which four thousand years have not exhausted. *A. B. Simpson.*

No man ever sank beneath the burden of the day! It is when tomorrow's burden is added to the burden of today that the weight is more than we can bear. It is delightfully easy to live one day at a time.

And he led them forth by the right way . . . (Psalm 107:7).

> Is this the right road home, O Lord?
>   The clouds are dark and still,
> The stony path is hard to tread.
>   Each step brings some fresh ill.
> I thought the way would brighter grow,
> And that the sun with warmth would glow,
> And joyous songs from free hearts flow.
>   Is *this* the right road home?
>
> Yes, child, this very path I trod,
>   The clouds were dark for me,
> The stony path was sharp and hard.
>   No sight, but faith could see
> That at the end the sun shines bright,
> Forever where there is no night,
> And glad hearts rest from earth's fierce fight.
>   It *is* the right road home!

The way of the cross leads home.

Moreover we know that to those who love God, who are called according to His Plan, everything that happens fits into a pattern for good (Rom. 8:28—Phillip's Trans.).

A t sixty years of age, Dr. R. B. Bingham was plunged through a windshield, virtually scalped, had broken bones, and was taken unconscious to a hospital. The next day he found himself there and inquired of the nurse what this was all about. She cautioned him to be quiet because he had had a terrible accident.

"Accident? Accident? There is no accident to a Christian; this is an incident!"

In his first sermon thereafter, Dr. Bingham said, "I have been through every translation in the English Bible and I cannot find anywhere that a Christian can experience an accident." He knew that for a Christian in the will of God, all circumstances are foreseen and permitted by a higher and holier wisdom. It was George Mueller who said, "Out of 1000 things that can come into a Christian's life, it is not 999 of them that work together for good, but 999 plus one!"

Trials when very heavy kill little people, but they make great ones.

. . . Help one another along the right road with your . . . Christian songs (Col. 3:16—Phillips' Trans.).

The man who broke into singing at midnight in the prison of Philippi when a few hours before he had been beaten with Roman thongs, has a very active sort of minstrelsy in his soul which would wake into music at the lightest touch of events.

At any rate, he strongly urges the use of singing as one of the inspiring helps in the spiritual life. In his letter to the Ephesians Paul recommends it as a substitute for wine! He counsels his readers not to seek their stimulus through the body, but through the spirit, not by the quickening of the flesh, but by the exaltation of the soul. If they seek spiritual stimulus they will have less need of material stimulant; the more of song, the less of wine! And who has not known the inspiration of song? Who has not known the stale flatness of some depressing scene lifted away by the ministry of song?

> Sometimes a light surprises
> The Christian when he sings.

Yes, and when the light breaks upon the soul, like some shaft of sunshine breaking through a cloudy day, the bird is apt to sing all the more, with the result that twilight passes into glorious day.

. . . My expectation is from Him . . . Thine expectation shall not be cut off
(Psalm 62:5, Prov. 23:18).

> Some glorious morn—but when? Ah, who shall say?
> The steepest mountain will become a plain,
> And the parched land be satisfied with rain,
> The gates of brass all broken; iron bars,
> Transfigured, form a ladder to the stars.
> Rough places plain, and crooked ways all straight
> For him who with a patient heart can wait
> These things shall be on God's appointed day
> It may not be tomorrow—yet it may.

Never doubt in the dark when God has spoken in the light.

Blessed are the peace-makers for they shall be called God's sons (Matt. 5:9—Berkeley Version).

It is very easy, if you are talking to one who has a little distrust of another or a little bitterness against another, to say a word which will increase the distrust or add to the bitterness. We like to approve and justify the one with whom we are speaking, and in doing so we are apt to confirm him in his bitterness or sense of wrong. Let us be on our guard that we do not unintentionally widen little rifts into great breaches. Let us seek ever to be peacemakers. There is no other beatitude whose blessing is more radiant than that of the peacemaker—"they shall be called sons of God."

Praised by my Lord for all those who pardon one another for His love's sake.

Let me be severe toward myself, tender toward others, and loving toward both.

. . . Encourage one another, day after day, so long as "today" lasts (Heb. 3:13—Weymouth).

> She had a doubt, and buried it
>   Before the day was old;
> She did not tell it to a friend—
>   What if his love grew cold?
>
> She buried it; and turned to Christ.
>   "Lord, Thou hast died for me—
> Increase my faith, my feeble faith,
>   And bid me cling to Thee!"

The days are always dark enough. There is no need for us to emphasize the fact by further spreading gloom. Instead we should seize every opportunity to give encouragement. George Matthew Adams tells us that encouragement is oxygen to the soul. A real test of Christian character is the atmosphere one carries around with him. Our lives *should radiate the joy and gratitude of our Christian experience so that others may be encouraged by our attitude.*

My covenant will I not break, nor alter the thing that is gone out of my lips (Psalm 89:34).

Neither of us ever worry," writes a man who had lost all in China. "We know how to cast our burdens upon the Lord who takes all the grind out of life. It is forty-two years ago this month since I first arrived in Kwangsi in His service and what years of mercy they have been. Not one word of His promise has failed. But, alas, how much failure on our part to grasp those promises and to act upon them as if we really believed them! *The words of a little boy come to me, "Do you really mean it, father, or is it only a promise?"*

The enemy shall not exact upon him; nor the son of wickedness afflict him (Psalm 89:22).

Let us seek the quiet heart in our prayers. Prayer must arise within us as a fountain from unknown depths. But we must leave it to God to answer in His own wisest way. We are so impatient, and think that God does not answer.

A child asked God for fine weather on her birthday, and it rained! Someone said, "God didn't answer your prayer."

"Oh, yes," she replied, "He did. God always answers, but He said No!"

God always answers! He never fails! Be still! If we abide in Him, and He abides in us, we ask what we will, and it is done. As a sound may dislodge an avalanche, so the prayer of faith sets in motion the power of God.

In times of difficulty—be still! Thine enemies are plotting thine overthrow! They laugh at thy strong confidence! But hast thou not heard His voice saying, "This is the way, walk ye in it." Then leave Him to deal with thy foes from whatever quarter they come. He is thy rock, and rocks do not shake. He is thy high tower, and a high tower cannot be flooded. Thou needest mercy, and to Him belongeth mercy. Do not run hither and thither in panic. Just quietly wait, hushing thy soul, as He did the fears of His friends on the eve of Gethsemane and Calvary.

Prayer is the opening of a channel from your emptiness to God's fullness.

And the Lord went before them by day in a pillar of a cloud, to lead them the way; and by night in a pillar of fire, to give them light; to go by day and night (Exod. 13:21).

The woods were dark and the night was black
And only an owl could see the track;
But the cheery driver made his way
Through the great pine woods as if it were day.

I asked him, "How do you manage to see?
The road and the forest are one to me."
"To me as well," he replied, "And I
Can only drive by the path in the sky."

I looked above, where the tree tops tall
Rose from the road, like an ebon wall;
And lo! a beautiful starry lane
Wound as the road wound and made it plain.

And since when the path of my life is drear,
And all is blackness and doubt and fear,
When the horrors of midnight are here below
And I see not a step of the way to go,
Then, oh! then, I can look on high
And walk on earth by the light in the sky.   *Amos R. Wells*

If we will walk with Christ in the sunshine, He will walk with us in the shadows.

Peter . . . saith to Jesus, Lord and what shall this man do? Jesus saith unto him . . . what is that to thee? follow thou me (John 21:21, 22).

There may be many dear saints of God who doubt their saintship because their activities have been taken from them. Circumstances have closed in upon them; doors have been shut in their faces; funds for the prosecution of their work have ceased. It may be that, physically exhausted, they lie on their beds wondering why He can consent to so unreasonable a situation.

Be assured of one thing, we are not to remain in obscurity and inactivity for all time. Our error lies in mentally fixing our future according to present conditions.

There is always the afterward of His gracious promising.

Rev. Kenneth MacKenzie.

I am the vine, ye are the branches; He that abideth in me, and I in him, the same bringeth forth much fruit; for without me ye can do nothing (John 15:5).

> O, struggle not to abide,
>   Nor labor to bring forth fruit,
> But let Jesus unite thee to Himself
>   As the vine branch to the root.
>
> So simple, so deep, so strong
>   That union with Him shall be,
> His life shall ever replace thine own
>   And His love shall flow through thee.
>   *Found written in Charles Cowman's Bible.*

Fruit comes from living in God. It is the result of His life flowing in us, of our yielding to His power; not of our trying and struggling to be good.

In the Waldensian Valleys in Italy some of the vines are grown on huge wooden crosses—and in September they are a beautiful sight laden with grapes. The branches are stretched out on the cross, and so get every drop of rain, every ray of sun. I do not suppose these branches are conscious of the cross, as much as they are of the warmth and life and joy of fruit bearing.

Is that not a parable of the Christian life? It explains the joy and peace of the early church, even in persecution. They had utterly given themselves to Another; self was crucified with Christ and joy and fruitfulness were the result, as it will be with us today, if our lives are hid with Christ in God.   *S. T. Fraser.*

Blessed are the gentle (God moulded, God tamed) for they shall inherit the earth (Matt. 5:5—Berkeley Version).

There are two nobilities. One is made up of the starred and gartered men who sweep their robes over marble halls and bend low at the sight and smile of the man in purple. But there is another nobility who live in lowlier houses, who plow our fields, work in our factories and care for the children at home; who love the Kingdom of Christ because of the love of their Ruler, who have never known their names to be written in human books, but know they are written on the Saviour's palm; whose deeds of sacrifice belong to a higher order than the canons of heraldry know, and whose patent to everlasting rank is their consecration of time and slender means and deepest soul to the beloved cause of the living Lord.

I plead for the rights of the unmarked nobility! I would say a word in advocacy of the many who cannot found a university, or erect a hall, or put an alcove in a library, whose marble busts will never ornament a gallery nor a public park, but whose faces are familiar to the angels because of what they do for the cause of Christ on earth.

Some men make a living; others make a life.

Now there was leaning on Jesus' bosom one of his disciples whom Jesus loved (John 13:23).

> It's not a mansion, Lord, I want so much
>   But just a little shelter where thine eye
> Can be upon me and keep in touch,
>   Where thou canst hear me, Lord, should I but cry.
>
> Lord, to be near Thee! Make so short a lane
>   Between my dwelling and the place Thou art
> That I may hasten there in joy or pain
>   To tell Thee all the things that fill my heart.
>
> No gate to bar me, neither wall nor stone
>   To stumble over, or to slow my pace,
> No thicket thorny, with weeds o'ergrown,
>   To hide the vision of Thy so loved face.
>
> Let me be near Thee, for I need it so!
>   However humble be my lot or task;
> This precious comfort, Lord, on me bestow—
>   Just to be near Thee, this is all I ask.

We are not only made "by" Christ, we are also made "for" Him. When we find Christ we find fulfillment. His will is our peace.

Christ and life are one, and we cannot live against Christ without living against life,

Now ye are clean through the word which I have spoken unto you (John 15:3).

I cannot tell," said the humblest shepherd's wife, "what sermon it was that led to my conversion. I cannot explain even the creed or the catechism, but I know that something has changed me. Last summer John and I washed the sheep in yonder stream. I cannot tell you where the water went, but I can show you the clean, white fleece of the sheep."

And so, I may forget the doctrines, but I have the blessed fruit in my heart and life.

A backwoods preacher who knew little of books or theology, but who had what was a vast deal better, a practical knowledge of salvation through Christ, was before a conference committee for examination. "Will you please name some of the evidences of the divinity of our Lord Jesus Christ?" said one of his wise examiners. The preacher's face wore an expression of puzzled bewilderment and he was silent. The examiner repeated his question, "What makes you think Christ is divine?" Now there was a response from the whole man! With tears in his eyes, he started to his feet and stretching out his arms and hands he exclaimed, *"How do I know He's divine? Why bless you, He's saved my soul and I love Him for it."*

I will sing unto the Lord as long as I live: I will sing praise to my God while I have my being (Psalm 104:33).

A little boy was watching the birds in a field. At length a little songster perched itself on the limb of a tree. As the boy prepared to throw a stone, the little bird began to sing.

Slowly the boy dropped the stone. He listened till the song had ceased, and watched the bird fly away.

"Why did you not stone him?" asked a gentleman.

"Couldn't," was the brief reply. "couldn't, 'cos he sung so."

Thus the enemy of our soul is on the lookout to fire some poisonous dart of doubt or fear. Sing, sing in the warfare. The trial may be fiery, the march may seem long; let the glory in your soul sing His praise. The devil will flee. He does not like songs of praise. The joy of the Lord is excellent equipment for the conflict.

Uncertainty is unfavorable to song.

My times are in Thy hand . . . (Psalm 31:15).

I f you quote this verse to the native of Congo, he will be forced to translate it in the gorgeous words, "All my life *why's, when's, where's,* and *wherefore's* are in God's Hand!"

> His tender hands have fashioned tiny things:
>   The wee blue petals of forget-me-nots;
> A drop of mist; an insect's tissue wings;
>   A poppy seed; a caterpillar's spots;
> The sensitive antennae of a bee;
>   Each amber globule of the desert sands . . .
> Then shall I fear when He has said to me,
>   "Thy days, my little one, are in my hands?"
>
> Vivian Ahrendt

There is nothing too hard for such a God.

I the Lord have called thee in righteousness and will hold thine hand and will keep thee and give thee for a covenant of the people, for a light of the Gentiles (Isa. 42:6).

O n the last day of her life, Francis Ridley Havergal had a friend read to her Isaiah 42. When verse 6 was read Miss Havergal stopped her, "Well, I will just go home on that." She whispered three words of the verse—"Called—held—kept," and soon expired.

> By an unfaltering trust approach thy end
> Like one who wraps the drapery of his couch about him
> And lies down to pleasant dreams.   *Bryant.*

Life is not measured by the time we live.

Call upon me in the day of trouble . . . (Psalm 50:15).

Once in an Eastern palace wide
  A little child sat weaving;
So patiently her task she plied,
The men and women at her side
  Flocked around her almost grieving.

"How is it, little one," they said,
  "You always work so cheerily?
You never seem to break your thread,
Or snarl or tangle it, instead
  Of working smooth and clearly."

"I only go and tell the King,"
  She said, abashed and meekly;
"You know He said, 'In everything.' "
"Why so do we!" they cried. "We bring
  Him all our troubles weekly."

She turned her little head aside;
  A moment let them wrangle;
"Ah, but," she softly then replied,
"I go and get the knot untied
  At the first little tangle!"

The story is told of a textile factory in which was found this sign on the wall over each machine: "If your threads get tangled, send for the foreman." A new employee went to work and soon the threads became badly tangled. The more she sought to untangle them, the more helpless she became. By and by in desperation, after wasting a lot of time, she did call for help. When the foreman came, he asked her why she had not sent for him earlier. She replied in self-defense, "I did my best." He *answered with a smile, "Remember, doing your best is sending for me."*

. . . O woman, great is thy faith . . . (Matt. 15:28).

O nly God is great in the superlative sense, and others are great in their relation to Him. Even so precious a thing as faith draws its principal force and effectiveness from its object. Therefore there is no great faith, except faith in God.

But even faith in a great God cannot be manifested except it have a background in circumstances. Faith must work, if it is to be revealed. Otherwise, it is abstract and potential, rather than concrete and real.

The woman of Tyre had a great and pressing need—her daughter was grievously vexed of the devil. She met great hindrances—the opposition of the disciples and the apparent indifference of the Lord Himself. She prayed a great prayer—she asked directly what she desired. She exercised great faith. To her the thing asked was insignificant in comparison to the ability of the One entreated. The hindrances were overshadowed by the glory of the Person approached. She obtained a great deliverance. A great need, a great hindrance, a great prayer, great faith and a great deliverance—a quintet of remarkables.

But the remarkable things of the Scriptures are not meant to be isolated—they are born to be contagious. We all have great needs. There are great hindrances to our prayers in all the realms that faith must explore, but we should come to God with courage. We should account Him faithful and should trust without the smallest admixture of doubt.

These things represent our part in the matter. That great deliverances will come to us is God's part in the matter. Nothing in all the realm of human experience is so sure as that God will keep His promise to those who obey Him.

. . . Our friend Lazarus sleepeth; but I go, that I may awake him out of sleep (John 11:11).

> Death is only an old door,
>   Set in a garden wall,
> On gentle hinges it gives at dusk
>   When the thrushes call.
>
> Along the lintel are green leaves,
>   Beyond the light lies still,
> Very willing and weary feet
>   Go over that sill.
>
> There is nothing to trouble any heart,
>   Nothing to hurt at all.
> Death is only a quiet door,
>   In an old wall.   *Nancy Byrd Turner.*

Jesus will pass through death's quiet door with His friend.

_____

. . . He will teach us of his ways and we will walk in his paths . . . (Isa. 2:3).

When holidays are holy days,
  And God shines everywhere,
We see Him in His works and ways,
  And know we meet Him there.
Happy the travelers on life's road
Who spend their holidays with God.

And some who have no holidays
  Have holy days instead;
In poor homes, and in lowly ways,
  Upon the sufferer's bed;
They walk no sunlit summer road,
But find their holidays in God.

May holidays and holy days,
  And every day be blessed;
And all God's people choose the ways
  That glorify Him best,
And make my days upon life's road
Real holy days with God.

We must expose ourselves to the circumstances of His choice.

. . . And she answered (the Shunammite woman who had lost her only son), It is well, (2 Kings 4:26).

During the dark hours of the rebellion, while the colored people were despondent and uncertain of their fate, one of their number, approaching General Grant, said, "How de do, Ginral Grant?" and extended his hand, which the General cordially shook. "How am tings goin', Ginral?" The General's reply was, "Everything is going right, sir." In a brief period the assuring words passed around the contraband camp, changing their despondency to hope and joy. *If the despondent Christian will go to his Commander, he may be assured, "Everything is going right."*

Who passing through the valley of Baca make it a well; the rain also filleth the pools (Psalm 84:6).

Have you ever been in the Valley of Baca? The clear translation of that word is "vale of misery." You certainly are familiar with that locality, for what human being is there who has not known misery at one time or another.

All men alike go into that shadowy, bleak valley. But how different they are when they come out. Some emerge from their suffering exhausted and beaten down, while others come out strengthened. These last are the folk who, "passing through the Vale of Misery use it for a well." In the Good News of God they have learned that days of sickness, of grief, of troubles, can be days of opportunity, days in which they find new springs of refreshment.

As a believing, practising Christian you can turn your particular vale into a well, and use it for strength. An older woman once told of the special miseries of old age, how they had brought her to an everyday quiet fifteen minutes with God—minutes in which she just listens in the stillness until the clouds clear a bit, and she sees, in the light of God's wisdom, how she can go on through the day. Your trial may be shortness of stature, a difficult husband, your own touchy disposition, painful rheumatism, slender finances, or too-many-people-in-one-house. Whatever it is, there are hidden springs in its barren wastes.

I have found forget-me-nots on many a rutty road. I have found wild roses behind a barricade of nettles.

God has no road without its springs. If His path stretches across the waste wilderness the "fountains shall break out in the desert, and the wilderness shall rejoice and blossom like the rose."

And thou shalt remember all the way which the Lord thy God led thee . . .
(Deut. 8:2).

Today I saw a slender locust tree
With misty white all sprinkled, as in May;
And giving forth to all who passed that way
Its delicate, rare fragrance lavishly.
The maples newly tipped with red might be;
The golden-rod in glowing waves might sway;
But the locust heeded not October's day—
It dressed itself for spring, and smiled at me.

Oh grant that when the autumn days of life
Shall come to me, my spirit then may bloom
And deck itself in white; recall its spring;
Remember battles won, forget the strife;
Forget old enemies, remember whom
It loved, be joyful in these thoughts—and sing!

Margaret Knowled Speidel.

What is there so beautiful as lovely old age? What does it matter
if the hair is white and the cheek has lost its bloom, if the eyes
shine with a heavenly light and one can fairly feel the faith that
lends its sweetness to the glance, its cadence to the voice.

Look not every man on his own things, but . . . on the things of others (Phil. 2:4).

S alute Apelles, approved in Christ." Nothing more is known of Apelles then this. It is enough. His was the ministry of the unnoticed—obscure, unseen, but approved.

We once knew a poor old man who trudged miles to repair the country stiles that they might be a little easier for the aged and infirm. The people voted him mentally strange but, in the Great Day he will outshine Napoleon.

To take a stumbling block out of our brother's way, and to help the cripple over the stile, is to reveal the mind that was in Christ Jesus.

. . . I have made and I will bear; even I will carry and will deliver you (Isa. 46:4).

The Vicar of St. Matthew's who visited Dr. J. H. Jowett during his last sickness says that Dr. Jowett said to him one day, "I said, 'Lord, I am one of the cavalry and I am laid low.' Then the Lord said to me, 'You are not one of the cavalry, you are one of My sheep.' "

We all need to be put into our right place in this way. To be one of the Lord's sheep is to be loved by Him, to be led by Him and to be dependent on Him in everything and all the time. The sheep can never do without its shepherd.

> The shepherd's bosom bears each lamb
>   O'er rock, and waste and wild:
> The object of that care I am—
>   I am the Shepherd's child.

He tempers the wind to the shorn lamb.

And he died in a good old age, full of days, riches and honor . . .
(1 Chron. 29:28).

> 'Tis yet high day, thy staff resume
> And fight fresh battles for the truth;
> For what is age, but youth's full bloom,
> A riper, more transcendent youth?
> A weight of gold
> Is never old.
> Streams broader grow as downward rolled.
>
> At sixty-two life has begun
> At seventy-three begins once more,
> Fly swifter as thou near'st the sun,
> And brighter shine at eighty-four.
> At ninety-five
> Shouldst thou arrive
> Still wait on God and work and thrive.   *Oliver W. Holmes*

I want to be thoroughly used up when I die, for the harder I work, the more I live. Life is no brief candle for me. It is a sort of splendid torch which I have got hold of for a moment, and I want to make it burn as brightly as possible before handing it on to future generations.   *Selected.*

His coming is as certain as the dawn (Amos 5:8—Arabic).

> Wide-flung, the rosy banners of the dawn
>   Blazon the eastern sky,
> A whisp'ring zephyr stirs the breathless trees
>   And passes by.
>
> Etched 'gainst the changing pageant
>   Clear stand the sombre pines.
> While all the low horizon, deeply gold,
>   With splendor shines.
>
> Wrapt in a fragrant stillness now the earth
>   Holds up her dew-washed face,
> Waiting the daily miracle of God,
>   His act of Grace.
>
> Then, in my list'ning heart, a still small voice,
>   These words I hear Him say:
> "Whose coming is as certain as the dawn,
>   Perhaps today."   *Ivy M. Fordham.*

And Thou wilt come with radiant angel train, Lord of the harvest, claiming all Thine own.

. . . Mine age is as nothing before Thee . . . (Psalm 39:5).

I s it not sad to grow old? Say rather it is a very difficult art, and one which few men have ever acquired. . . . To grow old is sad indeed if what you want is to hold back the receding years, to keep your hair from growing white, your eyes from becoming dim, and the wrinkles from chiseling their way across your brow.

One of the most beautiful things in the world is an old person, who, made better by experience, more indulgent, more charitable, loves mankind in spite of its wretchedness and adores youth without the slightest tendency to mimic it. Such a person is like an old Stradivarius whose tone has become so sweet that its value is increased a hundred-fold, and it seems almost to have a soul.

Charles Wagner.

> God give me sympathy and sense
>   And help me keep my courage high;
> God give me calm and confidence,
>   And—please—a twinkle in my eye.   *Margaret Bailey.*

Thank God for the smilers in the world.

. . . These hands have ministered unto my necessities, and to them that were with me (Acts 20:34).

One Thursday morning at the City Temple, Dr. Parker began his sermon by holding up a little vase of wild flowers. He said, "These flowers were gathered for me yesterday by little hands, in a Devonshire lane. Did I need them? No. Did I want them? Yes, a thousand times yes! God does not need our little services, but He wants them with all the longing of a parent for the affection of the child, and with all the pleasure afforded to man by the gift of flowers."

"I remember," says Dr. Jowett, "an incident in *Aurora Leigh*. Lucy Gresham, the poor seamstress, lay dying in an attic. Marian Erle, also a poor seamstress, was in the workroom with the other girls when she heard the news. Laying down her work at once, she hastened away to the sufferer that she might be God's minister in the hour of need. "Why God," thought Marian, "has a missing hand this moment; Lucy wants a drink, perhaps. Let others miss me! Never miss me, God."

"That willingness to be the missing hand," adds Dr. Parker, "is the secret and the genius of a consecrated life."

> If Thou dost need a hand today,
> To clasp another hand on life's rough way,
> Take mine, dear Lord, take mine.

. . . Let us run with patience the race that is set before us, Looking unto Jesus the author and finisher of our faith . . . (Heb. 12:1, 2).

The last mile of the road is perhaps the hardest bit to travel. When we reach the final lap we are apt to be weary and spent. It is not that we are discouraged; not that, even though the way at times has been difficult. It is only that we are tired and the evening has come and we long for rest.

We cannot be expected to strain forward to the end of things with the same throb of excitement and suspense that we felt when we were at the road's beginning. We cannot experience the young urge that we knew at the start of the race, when it was morning, and we were newly awakened. But though we cannot feel the old delightful tumult of pulse and brain, we can still cling to the thread of melody that has been our marching song. We can still sing very softly as our laggard feet carry us toward the place called Home.

Home! It is the last stanza of the road song. It is the meeting with beauty—not awful, appalling beauty, but the beauty of familiar scenes glorified, and dear, smiling faces we have lost awhile. It is the fulfillment of the road's promise, and the justification of the road's agony.

Home! It is the last stanza of the song and the end of the road. And—paradoxically, superbly—it is the beginning of a new song and the first step upon a road that has no ending.

Margaret Elizabeth Sangster.

*My voice shalt thou hear in the morning, O Lord; in the morning will I
direct my prayer unto thee and will look up! (Psalm 5:3).*

> A moment in the morning 'ere the cares of the day begin,
> 'Ere the heart's wide door is open for the world to enter
> in;
> Ah, then, alone with Jesus, in the silence of the morn,
> In heavenly sweet communion, let your happy day be
> born;
> In the quietude that blesses with a prelude of repose,
> Let your soul be soothed and softened as the dew revives
> the rose.

It was the habit of a devout servant of God to sit still before the
Lord for an unbroken period at the end of each day that he might
hear what God might speak. "Speak, Lord, for thy servant
heareth."

*Happy is the man who makes a daily parenthesis of silence in
his heart that he may hear God speaking.*

Ye that are the Lord's remembrancers, keep not silence (Isa. 62:6—RV).

O ne of the great stories of answered prayer is in connection with the work of Charles G. Finney. Wherever he went, after the power of God had come upon him for service, large numbers of people were being aroused to new earnestness, while greater numbers of people were being brought to repentance for sin, seeking and finding the Lord as their Saviour.

There was much talk about Mr. Finney. But behind Mr. Finney was his little-known friend, Mr. Abel Clary, a minister who gave himself to private prayer. He never appeared at the public gatherings; indeed he was in feeble health; but lying in the bed he would write in his journal: "My heart has been moved to pray for _____ (such and such towns)."

After Mr. Clary's death, Mr. Finney obtained this memorandum book, and found that *the precise order of the burden laid upon that man's heart, was the order of blessing as poured upon his own ministry.*

. . . When He hath tried me, I shall come forth as gold (Job 23:10).

> Forward I go! what future days may have
> In store for me, whatever be my cross,
> The mountain top, the valley, gain or loss,
> May I come forth pure as refiner's gold;
> All else but Christ to reckon worthless dross.

Dr. Stuart Holden told his congregation how, when he visited a factory in the North of England, where costly china was being made, the thing which interested him most was the painting on the finished product.

"It had been through many different processes, and was taken to the studio for the artists to complete. I saw the pattern being put on in various colors, and noticed that a great deal of black was being used. On asking why I was told, 'It is black now, but it will be gold when it comes out of the fire.'

"Is not this just as in our lives? What is put on black, we do not recognize as gold at the time, and the thing which is gilding our lives—or is intended to do so—is very often put on in darkness and blackness."

Wait for God's "afters."

. . . Let thine heart keep my commandments: for length of days and long life and peace shall they add to thee (Prov. 3:1, 2).

I t is in their autumn days that men see most clearly the purpose of life, in the clear light of a trained experience of its values. They can retire then at some distance from the world, and see it in its truer perspective. They learn how worthless are the objects of the bitterest contentions, how unsatisfactory are its prizes, how fickle are it favours. They see clearly with the contemplative interpretation of life's experience. That is one fruit to be gathered in a man's harvest time.

> So let the road wind up the hill or down,
> O'er rough or smooth, the journey will be joy;
> Still seeking what I sought when but a boy
> New friendship, high adventure and a crown.
> My heart will keep the courage of the quest,
> And hope the road's last turn will be best.

Old age can be the crown of man's life.

Wherever I go, thank God, he makes my life a constant pageant of triumph in Christ (2 Cor. 2:14—Modern Trans.).

A young man went to an aged saint on one occasion and asked him to pray for him, saying, "I find myself giving way to impatience continually. Will you please pray for me that I may be more patient?" The old man prayed, "Lord send this young man tribulation in the morning, send him tribulation in the afternoon. . . . " The young man nudged him saying, "No, no, not tribulation, patience." "But, " remonstrated the old saint, "it is tribulation that worketh patience! If you would know patience, you must have tribulation."

If you would know victory, you must have conflict; it is ridiculous for anybody to talk about having a victory when they have never been in conflict. You must be prepared to enter into the arena with the Lord Jesus Christ Himself, and He will give you lessons day by day. No one can enjoy victory without paying the price, even in the ordinary realms of life. If you would know what it is to triumph, you must certainly pass through tribulation. If you want patience, then it is tribulation; if you want victory there must be conflict.

The most difficult of tasks is to keep heights which the soul is competent to gain.

236

. . . I go to prepare a place for you (John 14:2).

An old man who was very ill, wrote the following of Heaven: "I am interested in Heaven because I have held a clear title to a bit of property there for over fifty-five years. I did not buy it. It was given to me without money and without price. But the donor purchased it for me at a tremendous sacrifice. I am not holding it for speculation since the title is not transferable. It is not a vacant lot. For more than half a century I have been sending materials out of which the greatest architect and builder of the universe has been building a home for me which will never need to be repaired because it will suit me perfectly, individually, and will never grow old. Termites can never undermine its foundations, for they rest upon the Rock of Ages. Fire cannot destory it. Floods cannot wash it away. No locks nor bolts will ever be placed upon its doors, for no vicious person can ever enter that land where my dwelling stands now almost completed and almost ready for me to enter in and abide in peace eternally without fear of being ejected.

"There is a valley of deep shadows between the place where I live and that to which I shall journey in a very short time. I cannot reach my home in that City of Gold without passing through this deep valley of shadows, but I am not afraid, because the best Friend I ever had went through the same valley long ago and drove away all of its gloom. He has stuck by me through thick and thin ever since we first became acquainted fifty-five years ago and I hold His promise in printed form, never to forsake nor leave me alone. *He will be with me as I walk through the valley of shadows and I shall not lose my way when He is with me.*"

The eyes of all wait upon thee; and thou givest them their meat in due season (Psalm 145:15).

A sick member of a congregation debarred from attending her customary place of worship, intrusted to the hand of the minister a two-shilling piece which he was to hand to a poor widow known to them both.

It so happened that the minister encountered the widow slowly making her way from the church and at once handed her the coin. He was hardly prepared for the immediate response, "I did not think that He would have sent it so soon." On further inquiry he discovered that she had placed her last coin that day in the collection, and was entirely dependent upon such answer as her heavenly Father might send to her trustful prayer that He would provide for her next meal.

Are we accustomed to such close dealings with God?

Rest in the Lord and wait patiently for him . . . (Psalm 37:7).

The late Bishop Moule has told how once, during the war, at the close of an entertainment given for men going out to the front, a young officer arose at his Colonel's request to express the thanks of the men. He did so in genial words of charm and humor. Then suddenly, as if in afterthought, and in a different tone, he added: "We are soon crossing to France and to the trenches, and very possibly, of course, to death. Will any of our friends here tell us how to die?"

There was a long, strained silence. Then the answer came. One of the singers made her way quietly forward to the front of the stage and began to sing the great *Aria from Elijah,* "O rest in the Lord." There were few dry eyes when the song was concluded.

Here, above all else, is what each one of us needs in the battle of life: a heart that has come to rest in God; a will fully surrendered. That is the great secret. That, alone, will bring us through with honor.   *James Stewart.*

> And when the strife is fierce, the warfare long,
> Steals on the ear the distant triumph song,
> And hearts are brave again, and arms are strong.

The music of the Gospel leads us Home!

. . . Blessed are the dead which die in the Lord . . . that they may rest from their labors; and their works do follow them (Rev. 14:13).

E dwin Markham's greatest enthusiasm was for immortality. The closing lines from his poem, "Anchored to the Infinite," read:

> So may we send our little timid thought
> Across the void, out to God's reaching hands—
> Send out our love and faith to thread the deep—
> Thought after thought until the little cord
> Has greatened to a chain no chance can break,
> And we are anchored to the Infinite.

This grand old man, and intellectual giant in one, took the future life as much for granted as he did his daily food. "The future life is where we will go on helping to bring the universe to perfection, which is His grand ultimate aim," he once said. When asked what is the purpose of life, he immediately replied, "To help God run the universe. Every Christian in that better land will be busy all the time, and the environment will be perfect all the time for doing the work which God assigns to all."

Courage! 'Tis never so far from a plodded path to a shining star!

. . . To give unto them . . . the garment of praise for the spirit of heaviness . . . (Isa. 61:3).

Thy feelings will ebb and flow, thy heart will grow warm in summer's glow, and cold in winter's chill, thou wilt be brave and steadfast today, downcast and anxious tomorrow. Thy streams will be full in the rainy season, and in the time of drought they will be bare beds of stone.

Turn away from thyself! Hope in God! He fainteth not neither is weary. He is the unfailing fountain; His affections do not decay; with Him is no variableness, neither shadow of turning. When thou are dismayed, He is still full of eternal peace. When thou art downcast, He is still untroubled.

It is impossible to keep cares from flocking in great swarms around us, but it is our fault if they are allowed to make nests in our hearts.

. . . I am with thee to deliver thee, saith the Lord (Jer. 1:8).

God does not grant the necessary grace before the trial. He builds the bridge when we reach the river. We often fear that we shall sink under the fiery trials that we see others endure. We are afraid in the distance of the mystery and anguish of death; but we have not yet reached that crisis, and grace is not vouchsafed before it is needed. Jesus comes with our distress.

God does not save us from facing the music, or shelter us from any of the requirements of sons and daughters. As long as we remain within the moral frontiers of God, watching our hearts lest we give way to ill-content, to covetousness, or self pity, the things which take us outside God's frontier, then God says, "I will in no wise fail thee, neither will I in any wise forsake thee."

An aged Christian when asked if he ever feared death replied, "Yes, I sometimes tremble on the Rock, but the Rock never trembles under me."

Then they willingly received Him into the ship, and immediately the ship was at the land whither they went (John 6:21).

We need more immediateness in prayer. So many prayers are offered in a spirit which really says, "I will not be grieved if the answer does not come soon; and, in fact, if it does not come at all, I will not be greatly disappointed."

There is so little real urgency in many prayers that the petitions amount to little more than a pious wish. The possibilities of importunity in prayer are mostly forgotten. Importunity pleads for immediateness.

It is a spur to faith to look at some of the "immediates" in the New Testament. In Mark's Gospel there are at least forty: "Immediately the fever left her," "Immediately the leprosy departed," "Immediately he received his sight."

The fervent prayer of the persecuted Christians brought the sudden answer in the conversion of Saul of Tarsus.

Paul and Silas in prison at Philippi received a sudden and immediate answer.

Although there are many prayers that will receive gradual answers, we are sure that there are thousands of others that will be immediately answered provided there is faith for God's immediate working.

. . . Jesus Christ . . . hath abolished death and hath brought life and immortality to light through the Gospel (2 Tim. 1:10).

> Would you be young again,
>   So would not I;
> One tear to mem'ry given,
>   Onward I'd hie.
> Life's dark flood forded o'er
>   All but at rest on shore,
> Say, would you plunge once more
>   With Home so nigh?
>
> If you might, would you now
>   Retrace your way?
> Wander through stormy wilds
>   Faint and astray?
> Night's gloomy watches spread,
>   Morning all beaming red,
> Hope's smiles around us shed,
>   Heavenward away!

God is forever and forever beginning again. He is forever and forever getting new mornings out of old nights, fair beginnings out of dismal endings.

. . . For since the beginning of the world, men have not heard nor perceived by the ear, neither hath the eye seen, O God, beside thee, what he hath prepared for him that waiteth for him (Isa. 64:4).

An old Indian chief, who lived in a great forest at the foot of a lofty mountain peak summoned the lads of the tribe to his side and commanded them to climb to the top of the lofty mountain peak and win renown for themselves, thus testing their mettle and proving their worth to the tribe.

Hours passed before one returned bringing a tuft of moss from the mountain's side; another brought a twig of a tree from still higher up the mountain; a third grasped a beautiful flower which grew near the summit.

As night began to fall, the last climber stepped into the firelight. Had he conquered the peak? No need to ask. His face was lighted with the glory of the vision as he cried, "I have seen the crystal sea."

Life is eternal, love is immortal, death is only a horizon, and a horizon is only the limit of our sight.

There shall not any man be able to stand before thee all the days of thy life; as I was with Moses, so I will be with thee; I will not fail thee nor forsake thee (Josh. 1:5).

We may be called to traverse strange ways, but we shall always have our Lord's company, assistance and provision. We need not covet money, for we shall always have our God, and He is better than gold; His favor is better then fortune.

We must imitate Alpine climbers and keep strong hold of the guide as we climb toward the top. Let us take short views. If we look over precipices, we shall grow dizzy. If we look to far ahead, we shall grow discouraged. Let us rather put our weak hands into Christ's strong loving grasp, and all the time listen to His cheering words, "Fear not, only trust!"   *Theodore L. Cuyler*

Learn the art of drawing a little curtain over the future.

. . . For the former things are passed away, and he that sat upon the throne said, Behold I make all things new . . . (Rev. 21:4-5).

Run familiarly through the streets of the heavenly Jerusalem; visit the patriarchs and prophets; salute the apostles and admire the armies of martyrs; lead on the heart from street to street; bring it into the palace of the Great King; lead it, as it were from chamber to chamber. Say to it: Here must I lodge, here must I die, here must I praise, here must I love and be loved. My tears will then be wiped away, my groans be turned to another tune, my cottage of clay be changed to this palace, my prison rags to these splendid robes; for the former things are passed away!

Richard Baxter.

No future can guarantee my present, but my present is a guarantee of my future.

I will awake the dawn (Psalm 57:8—Smith's Trans.).

> I am alone. The morning breaks
>   And all is quiet here;
> I need but lift my eyes, put forth
>   My hand, for God is near.
> Into this blissful, holy calm
>   No voice or harsh sound breaks.
> I am content. Enough to be
>   With Him, when morn awakes.   *Kate Browning Pfantz.*

How unspeakably great and wonderful is this early time with God before each day! Prepare for the day early, before the world around you is awake or stirring. The hour before the dawn is the hour of renewal; throughout the day the stillness of the early dawn will remain as a blessing. In the stillness open your heart; let God reign in your soul. Make your devotion as simple and as fragrant as the wild rose blooming alone in the wood, just because it is a wild rose and God made it so!

Reach up as far as you can and God will reach down all the rest of the way.

. . . In quietness and in confidence shall be your strength . . . but ye said, No; for we will flee upon horses . . . (Isa. 30:15-16).

The wild desire to be forever racing against old Father Time is one of the kill joys of modern life. The ancient traveler is sure to beat you in the long run and as long as you are trying to rival him, he will make your life a burden. But, if you will only acknowledge his superiority and profess that you do not approve of racing after all, he will settle down quietly beside you and jog along like the most companionable of creatures. *It is a pleasant pilgrimage in which the journey itself is part of the destination.*

Jesus, however, habitually withdrew into the desert for prayer (Luke 5:16—Berkeley Version).

The mountains and the desert—the two most lonely places on earth—were the constant resorts of our blessed Lord. All his public work, all his active labors, were blended with them. It was seemly and befitting that the Lord of Creation should have the stillness of the desert and the solitude of the mountain-top as His closet.

Traveling in His own thoughts, at a height to which none could approach, misunderstood by all and sympathized with by few, He must have felt Himself alone. It belongs to everything that soars above the common level to undergo the penalty of loneliness; and He knew pre-eminently what it was.

The desert has always been a great part of God's apportionment for His children. How many pages of God's Word are devoted to these records of the desert. Moses spent forty years there. Elijah, John the Baptist, Paul, Philip, all were led into the desert to learn lessons that could only be learned there. Israel's lifetime is filled up with records of the desert. All teach us how needful it is that our public life should be full of wilderness records. All life is superficial without it. All character lacks reality that has not much of such training. God provides solitude for us all, and for the same reason as He provided it for His people of old—to know Him, to know themselves, and to fit them for His service. *Frederick Whitfield.*

Silence is a great peacemaker.

Thy way is in the sea, and thy path in the great waters . . . (Psalm 77:19).

G od's path is in the sea—just where you would expect it to be! So when He leads us out by unexpected ways, off the strong solid land, out upon the changing sea, then we may expect to see His ways. We are with One who finds a path as He goes. That is better than having a path already tracked out, for it makes us perfectly independent of circumstances.

There is an infinite variety in the paths God makes, and He can make them anywhere. Think you not that He who made the spider able to drop anywhere and to spin its own path as it goes, is not able to spin a path for you through every blank, or perplexity, or depression? *C. A. Fox.*

We are but passengers on the voyage of life. The pilot understands the way. His eyes are always ahead. He will be the last to leave his post in time of danger.

_____

My soul shall be joyful in the Lord; it shall rejoice in his salvation (Psalm 35:9).

It is said that a friend once asked the great composer Haydn why his church music was always so full of gladness. He answered, "I cannot make it otherwise. I write according to the thoughts I feel; when I think upon my God, my heart is so full of joy that the notes dance and leap from my pen; and since God has given me a cheerful heart, it will be pardoned me that I serve him with a cheerful spirit."

Pardoned? Nay, it will be praised and rewarded. For God looks with approval, and man turns with gratitude to every one who shows by a cheerful heart that religion is a blessing for this world and the next.

Songs shorten the longest, darkest night.

Thine age shall be clearer than the noonday; thou shalt shine forth, thou shalt be as the morning (Job 11:17).

Age is a quality of mind—
If you have left your dreams behind,
If hope is lost,
If you no longer look ahead,
If your ambitions' fires are dead—
    Then you are old.

But if from life you take the best
And if in life you keep the jest,
If love you hold—
No matter how the years go by,
No matter how the birthdays fly,
    You are not old!

Nature does not die drably; she puts on her most gorgeous robes in autumn and then dies gloriously. She goes down with her gay banners waving.

We can face approaching age with serenity and make the last years the most beautiful.

. . . They shall mount up with wings . . . (Isa. 40:31).

My religious organs have been ailing for awhile past. I have lain a sheer hulk in consequence. But I got out my wings and have taken a change of air.

We travel along our roads as mere pedestrians, and we are sorely overcome, for the hostility of our circumstances wearies us to the dust. Or we are engaged upon some exacting ministry which imprisons us in our particular place. Or maybe we are shut up in a chamber of sickness, either as a patient, or in service upon the patient. In a hundred different ways we can be cribbed, cabined and confined and our religious organs are in danger of becoming sickly, and of losing their brightness both in mood and discernment.

All the time our wings are waiting. If we would, we could soar into larger regions in an ampler air. We have held too much the conception of the pilgrims and have kept too close to the road. We are the birds of God endowed with power to mount up with wings as eagles, to respond to the upward calling, and to breathe the lofty air of the heavenlies.

The crusaders who wage the noblest conflicts along the road, are those who get out their wings and soar for a change of air.

When we turn our hearts to the Lord, the power of wing is ours and we can rise from our little prisons, or from our tiresome road into the high heaven of spiritual rest and vision. *In the Christian life, rising is resting.* These wings are waiting for us.

Before I was afflicted, I went astray, but now have I kept thy word (Psalm 119:67).

A master of metaphor has made the complaining wax speak thus:

"Unaccountable this!" said the wax as from the flame it dropped melting upon the paper beneath.

"Do not grieve," said the paper, "I am sure it is all right!"

"I was never in such agony!" exclaimed the wax, still dropping.

"It is not without a good design, and will end well," replied the paper.

The wax was unable to reply at once, and when it again looked up it bore a beautiful impression, the counterpart of the seal which had been applied to it.

"Ah, I understand now!" said the wax, no longer in suffering. "I was softened in order to receive this lovely, durable impress."

God has made affliction as a morning shower to a green pasture, and as wick for His lamp, whereby earth and heaven are illumined.

. . . All thy waves and thy billows are gone over me. Yet the Lord will command His lovingkindness in the daytime, and in the night, His song shall be with me, and my prayer unto the God of my life (Psalm 42:7, 8).

S omeone once wrote that the man who can sing, "It is Well with My Soul" at a time in his life when "sorrows like sea billows roll," has learned the secret of the Lord, and can faithfully exclaim with Job, "Though He slay me, yet will I trust Him."

Such a man was Horatio Spafford, a lawyer in Chicago. When the great fire swept the city in 1871, he lost all his material possessions. Two years later, he sent his wife and four children to Europe, while he applied himself to retrieving his lost fortune.

They sailed on November 15, 1873, on the "S. S. Ville de Havre." In mid-ocean, one afternoon, six days after they had left New York, the ship collided with a sailing vessel.

Gathering her children on deck, immediately after the collision, Mrs. Spafford knelt in prayer, asking God to save them, or make them willing to die, if that were necessary. In fifteen minutes the boat sank! They were cast into the water and separated. Mrs. Spafford was taken out of the water unconscious by one of the oarsmen on duty in a lifeboat, but the children were lost.

Then days later Mrs. Spafford landed in Cardiff, Wales, and cabled to her husband, "Saved alone."

On receiving this terrible news Attorney Spafford exclaimed: "It is well; the will of the Lord be done!" To give expression to this faith he wrote the hymn which has blessed so many souls in deep trouble:

> When peace like a river attendeth my way,
>   When sorrows like sea-billows roll,
> Whatever my lot, thou hast taught me to say,
>   "It is well, it is well with my soul."

A wealthy man ruined in the panic of 1899 was giving himself up in despair, when a friend of his related to him the story of the writing of this hymn. Immediately he responded, "If Spafford could write such a beautiful resignation hymn, I shall never complain again."

. . . The husbandman waiteth for the precious fruit of the earth and hath long patience for it . . . (James 5:7).

I wish," said Dr. James Culross when dying, "that I could return just once more to my pulpit. I would preach on patience—'Be patient, therefore, brethren'—and I would have three heads to my discourse: Be very patient, I would say, with yourselves! Be very patient with each other. And be very patient with God."

> My soul, sit thou a patient looker-on;
> Judge not the Play before the Play is done;
> Her plot has many changes; every day
> Speaks a new scene; the last act crowns the Play.

We have so much patience with ourselves, why not borrow some of that and use it on others.

Come unto me and I will refresh you (Matt. 11:28—Modern Trans.).

Tell me about the Master!
  I am weary and worn tonight.
The day lies behind me in shadow,
  And only the evening is light.
Light with a radiant glory
  That lingers about the west,
My poor heart is aweary, aweary,
  And longs like a child for rest.

Tell me about the Master!
  Of the wrong He freely forgave,
Of His love and tender compassion,
  Of His love that is mighty to save.
For my heart is aweary, aweary,
  Of His woes and temptations of life,
Of the error that stalks in the noonday,
  Of falsehoods and malice and strife.

Yet, I know that whatever of sorrow,
  Or pain or temptation befall,
The Infinite Master has suffered,
  And knoweth and pitieth all.
So tell me the old, old story
  That falls on each wound like a balm,
And my heart that was burdened and broken
  Shall grow patient, and calm, and strong.

God is His own equivalent, and He needs nothing but Himself to achieve the great purposes on which He has set His heart.

Abundant living is not man's responsibility, but his response to God's ability.

Behold God exalteth by his power: Who teacheth like Him? (Job 36:22).

A man who had preserved his youth, not only in appearance, but in heart long after he had reached the limit of three score and ten, gave as his reason, "I have always looked forward to each new day eagerly. I know there will be something in it for me to learn, to enjoy. There will be unexpected blessings and surprises. There will be trials—perhaps sorrow—but I have learned to look upon them all as lessons which must be learned to look upon them all as lessons which must be learned in this school of life. I do not shrink from them now, but I welcome them as friends. Every day there come chances for putting happiness into the lives of others, opportunities large and small for serving my Master. And some day I will come face to face with 'The Great Adventure.' My Saviour will call me home. I cannot tell what day it will be; but I greet every new day with joy, for I know by experience that it will hold for me something good."

Anne Guilbert Mahon.

My country is not yesterday; my country is tomorrow.

And this is the confidence that we have in him, that if we ask anything according to his will, he heareth us; and if we know that he hear us, whatsoever we ask, we know that we have the petitions that we desired of him (1 John 5:14, 15).

I remember asking an old friend of mine, who is now between seventy and eighty years of age, and who, I think, as far as I have been permitted to know Christian men, is mightier with God than almost any man I have met, "Do tell me the secret of your success in prayer."

He said, "I will tell you what it is. I say to myself, "Is that which I am asking for promised? Is it according to the mind of God. If it is, I plant my foot upon it as upon a firm rock, and I never allow myself to doubt that my Father will give me according to my petition."   *Bishop E. H. Bickersteth.*

Every day we should have some new word of God to rest upon. How can God say no, to something He has promised?

. . . When thou hast shut thy door . . . (Matt. 6:6).

Dean Farrar says that his mother had the habit of retiring every morning for one hour, after breakfast, to her own room and there reading the Bible with meditation and prayer. From that hour, as from a great fountain, she drew strength and sweetness. He says he never saw her temper disturbed, nor heard her speak a word of anger or idle gossip. Her life was strong, pure, rich and full of blessing and healing; and he says it was all due to that daily morning hour with God.

The Master always kept a space of silence around His soul; that inner serenity which is, perhaps, one of the most important things a busy life can possess.

> Lord I have shut my door,
> Shut out life's busy cares and fretting noise,
> Here in this silence, they intrude no more.
> Speak Thou and heavenly joys
> Shall fill my heart with music sweet and calm,
>   A holy Psalm.
>
> Lord, I have shut my door!
> Come Thou and visit me; I am alone!
> Come as when doors were shut Thou cam'st of yore,
> And visited thine own!
> My Lord I kneel with reverent love and fear
>   For Thou art here!

The Lord is nigh unto them that are of a broken heart . . . (Psalm 34:18).

What broke your heart? Unkindness? Desertion? Unfaithfulness on the part of those you trusted? Or did you attempt to do something beyond your power, and in the effort the heart strings snapped? A bird with a broken wing, an animal with a broken leg, a woman with a broken heart, and man with a broken purpose in his life—these seem to drop out of the main current of life into shadow. They go apart to suffer and droop. The busy rush of life goes on without them. But God draws nigh. The Great Lover of man is always at His best when the lights burn low and dim in the house of life. He always comes to us then. He still sits as the Refiner. Where do you see love reflected? Not between the father and the stalwart son who counts himself independent or between the mother and the girl whose love is awakening in its first faint blush; but where the crippled child of eleven lies in the trundle bed, pale and wan, unable to help herself. There the noblest fruits of love ripen and yield refreshment. The father draws nigh to the little sufferer as soon as he gets home at night and the mother is near all the time, to sympathize and comfort and minister. So brokenness attracts God. It is dark; you think yourself deserted; but it is not so. God is there. He is nigh—call to Him. A whisper will bring a response.   *F. B. Meyer.*

None but Christ could ever accept a bird with a broken wing.

Now therefore give me this mountain . . . (Josh. 14:12—spoken by Caleb when he was eighty-five years old).

S omewhere near the snowy summit of the Alps there is an inscription that marks the last resting place of an Alpine guide. Just three short words tell the story, "He died climbing."

We often hear it said that such an one is "growing old." But as a matter of fact we do not grow old. We only get old when we cease to grow and climb.

Youth is essentially of the spirit, not of the calendar. To have made the climb of life is to have proved that while winter may be on the head, eternal youth is still within the heart.

We may be sixty, or seventy, or eighty years young.

Blessed is he, whosoever shall not be offended in Me (Matt. 11:6).

> Blessed is he, who through long years of suffering,
>   Cut off from active toil,
> Still shares by prayer and praise the work of others,
>   And thus divides the spoil.
>
> Blessed art thou, O child of God who sufferest,
>   And canst not understand
> The reason for thy pain, yet gladly leavest
>   Thy life in His blest Hand.
>
> Yea, blessed art thou, whose faith is "not offended"
>   By trials unexplained,
> By mysteries unsolved, past understanding
>   Until the goal is gained.
>
> For thee awaits an "afterward" of glory,
>   Eternal bliss complete,
> An understanding of His purpose for thee,
>   A joy exceeding sweet,
>
> The "unoffended" faith that here has trusted
>   A Father's boundless love,
> Shall then, made manifest in all its beauty,
>   Be crowned for aye above.

An old saint had a weather vane over his mission hall on which were the words, "God is love." When asked why he had put it there, his very suggestive reply was, "Why I want people to know that God is love whichever way the wind blows."

. . . Green pastures . . . still waters . . . (Psalm 23:2).

I traveled along a broad highway, where there was so much dust and tumult that my soul became weary . . . I was hurried forward by the tumultuous crowd. Then my heavenly Friend sought me in the throng, led me forth by secret ways, and brought me into a green meadow, and by still waters.

"In quietness and in confidence shall be your strength," says the prophet. There is a power in this rest in God, of which the men who are rushing along the broad and dusty highway can form no conception.

The path of those who have found the only good Shepherd leads indeed through a narrow and rocky valley . . . so that the light of the sun can no longer shine upon the road, but I know, although I cannot behold it, that the sun is shining. He is with me.

L. L.

I am not too small for God's attention.

Jesus said unto her, I am the resurrection, and the life: he that believeth in me, though he were dead, yet shall he live (John 11:25).

How gloriously God puts his maples to sleep! Did ever such color gladden the mind of the painter as is poured out on our hillsides and woods in autumn.

God made the world beautiful with a beauty beyond man's dream. He gave the wheat to keep us alive, but He gave the rose to feed our fancy, and even when He made the tree for the service of man, He made it with such wonderful shapeliness—such beautiful suggestiveness of stately column and fretted roof—as makes it cathedral-like in grandeur.

The maple leaf bears the print of His unrivaled pencil. His fingers touch the tree tops till they blush into a transfiguration beauty.

We fade as a leaf. Thank God if in such glory as this we make our exodus. *For the leaf fades gloriously—and in its fading it reveals God and it will reappear in resurrection vigor and fairness next Spring.*

There are diversities of operations, but it is the same God which worketh all in all (1 Cor. 12:6).

A n aged pilgrim and brother in the faith thus expresses himself with reference to his work: "Friends sometimes tell me I am too old for this or that, but the Spirit within me tells me that so long as He gives me health and mind, I am not to quit working for His Kingdom. From the time we are born into the Kingdom, until we hear the final summons to come Home, the great question before us should be working for the Eternal Kingdom. No one is too young; no one too old; let all labor, united in hand and heart, soul and spirit, having an eye single to the glory of God. Thank God for young workers, just coming in the field. Thank God for aged pilgrims, wide awake, pressing onward, giving us the benefit of their experience and ripened judgment."

Some lives, like evening primroses, blossom most beautifully in the evening of life.

The Lord will perfect that which concerneth me . . . (Psalm 138:8).

A ssured hope keeps the heart young. Life is ever at the dawn. Life is continuously at a beginning. It is always morning. One cannot be discouraged no matter how long, or hard, or wearisome the way; one keeps right on climbing—for he knows the path leads not only somewhere, but to the Everywhere, He knows he shall arrive.

> The day's long work is done, the west is red,
> The plough stands still, the gathered sheep are fed;
> And I, the Master's servant, turn and come
> From furrowed field, and pastoral upland, home;
> Home, 'neath the vesper star to still repose,
> Home—on the sounds of day the door to close,
> Home, to the twilight home of peace and prayer,
> Home—but a servant still, to meet my Master there!

An old Quaker, at eighty-two, with a beautiful face said, "I am going to live until I die, and then I'm going to live forever."

All things are delivered unto me of my Father; and no man knoweth the Son, but the Father; neither knoweth any man the Father, save the Son, and he to whomsoever the Son will reveal him (Matt. 11:27).

Charles Garnett of Liverpool was converted at an infidel lecture. "Christ," said the lecturer, "is a myth; now does anyone want to ask questions?"

An old woman of seventy-two arose and said, "I do. What is a myth?" "Nothing," he said. "You mean that Christ is nothing?" she asked. "Well, I will tell you my experience. I was left a widow with seven boys, without a penny in God's world. You say He is a myth. I brought up seven boys on that myth. He has clothed them every one. He has fed them day by day. They are now working for the Christ that brought them up, and the poorest of them is a better man than thou art."

That testimony convinced Charles Garnett that Christ is what He said He was.

> Let one more attest
> I have seen God's Hand
> Through a lifetime
> And all was for best.   *Robert Browning.*

. . . There is no discharge in that war . . . (Eccl. 8:8).

Years ago Sir. Wm. Robertson Nicol showed in a remarkable article that men died within eighteen months of their retirement because, having no hobby, they lost the zest of life that had been borne up in their life of labor. A famous insurance company doctor explained that men who retire don't live long because they are not prepared for leisure and it is a shock to them. Idleness is the greatest enemy of the aged and may easily present them with their ticket to death.

> Our tasks may glow with jewels or scintillate like gems,
> But once their motive is withdrawn, the deadly ebb begins;
> We call it "hardened arteries," "pneumonia," and "flu,"
> But men will die of "heartbreak," when they've nothing left to do.

Each stage of life has something peculiar to itself in possibility and achievement. To be victorious at each stage one must accept the fact of change and make out of that particular period through which he is passing something beautiful and effective.

Take courage in the words of a well-known psychiatrist, "I have never seen a case of mental disease in the aged where they have a faith in God, are free from the fear of death, and are active."

The hoary head is a crown of glory, if it be found in the way of righteousness (Prov. 16:31).

A gentleman writing about the breaking up of old ships, recently said that it is not age alone which improves the quality of the fiber in the wood of an old vessel, but the straining and wrenching of the vessel by the sea, the chemical action of the bilge water, and of many kinds of cargoes.

Some planks and veneers made from an oak beam which had been part of a ship eighty years old were exhibited a few years ago at a fashionable furniture store on Broadway in New York, and attracted general notice for the exquisite coloring and beautiful grain.

Equally striking were some beams of mahogany taken from a bark which sailed the seas sixty years ago. The years and the traffic had contracted the pores and deepened the color, until it looked as superb in its chromatic intensity as an antique Chinese vase. It was made into a cabinet and has today a place of honor in the drawing room of a wealthy New York family.

So there is a vast difference between the quality of old people who have lived flabby, self-indulgent, useless lives, and the fiber of those who have sailed all seas and carried all cargoes as the servants of God and the helpers of their fellow men.

Not only the wrenching and straining of life, but also something of the sweetness of the cargoes carried get into the very pores and fiber of character. Louis Albert Banks.

For by him were all things created, that are in heaven, and that are in earth . . . all things were created by him, and for him (Col. 1:16).

I was tired and sat down under the shadows of the great pines in a Swedish forest, glad to find such a cool retreat from the broiling sun. I had not been there long before I noticed a fragrant odor and wondered what it could be and where it came from.

No Marechal Niel rose grew on that barren soil, nor could the sun penetrate the shades of the forest to extract its perfume even if it had; I looked around, and found by my side a tiny flower about half the size of an ordinary daisy, nearly hidden from view by the moss. It was the little "Linea blomma."

Oh, how fragrant it smelled. Again and again I held it near my face, enjoying the perfume, and then I looked up and thanked God for that tiny flower, so insignificant, growing in a wild, almost untrodden forest, yet bringing cheer and refreshment to me.

I thought, why is it so obscure, when it is a flower with such fragrance, and surely worthy of a place in the most stately grounds? I learned a lesson by it, and it spoke powerfully to my heart.

I thought, if I cannot be a pine in God's forest, I may be a tiny flower to send forth the fragrance of Jesus in this world of sadness.

And they that know thy name will put their trust in thee: for thou, Lord, hast not forsaken them that seek thee (Psalm 9:10).

> Lord, give me faith!—to live from day to day,
> With tranquil heart to do my simple part,
> And, with my hand in thine, just go Thy way.
>
> Lord, give me faith—to trust, if not to know;
> With quiet mind in all things Thee to find,
> And child-like, go where Thou wouldst have me go.
>
> Lord, give me faith!—to leave it all to Thee,
> The future is thy gift, I would not lift
> The veil Thy love has hung 'twixt it and me.   *J. O.*

Lord, we would learn to trust in Thee at all times. We think we are trusting Thee when the sunlight falls unbroken and bright upon our way; but when the clouds gather and the storm breaks, our hearts faint and our faith loses its vision. May we have such faith as will feel Thee in the dark and walk calmly through the storm. We would learn when we are weary and fretful or tempted and discouraged to be still and know that Thou art God. May we cease our struggling and worrying and let Thee have Thy way with us until around our restfulness flows thy rest. But may such rest renew our vigor that we may fight the good fight of faith and win the victory. Amen.

> When obstacles and trials seem
> Like prison walls to be,
> I do the little I can do,
> And leave the rest to Thee.   *F. W. F.*

For he maketh sore, and bindeth up: he woundeth, and his hands make whole (Job 5:18).

S orrows are too precious to be wasted. That great man of God in the past generation, Alexander MacLaren of Manchester, used to bring out this over-looked truth. He reminded God's people that sorrows will, if we let them, "blow us to His breast, as a strong wind might sweep a man into some refuge from itself." I am sure there are many who can thankfully attest that they were brought nearer to God by some short, sharp sorrow, than by long days of prosperity. Take care that you do not waste your sorrows; that you do not let the precious gifts of disappointment, pain, loss, loneliness, ill health, or similar afflictions that come into your daily life mar you instead of mend you. See that they send you nearer to God and not that they drive you farther from Him.

They rest in God's will who have consecrated all to His use, even to their griefs. To such, indeed, He giveth songs in the night, dark though it be, and voice of the faintest star. Their cares are links with Heaven; singing they build their Bethel from the very stones of sorrow. *Hugh Redwood.*

In acceptance lieth peace.

. . . What I do thou knowest not now; but thou shalt know hereafter (John 13:7).

If we could see beyond today
  As God can see;
If all the clouds should roll away,
  The shadows flee,
O'er present griefs we would not fret,
Each sorrow we should soon forget,
For many joys are waiting yet,
  For you and me.

If we could know beyond today,
  As God doth know,
Why dearest treasures pass away
  And tears must flow,
And why the darkness leads to light,
Why dreary paths will soon grow bright!
Some day life's wrongs will be made right,
  Faith tells us so.

If we could see, if we could know,
  We often say.
But God in love a veil doth throw
  Across our way;
We cannot see what lies before,
And so we cling to Him the more;
He leads us till this life is o'er.
  Trust and obey.

Life is not one uniform leaden sky loaded with weeping clouds; the darkest horizon is rainbow-spanned; the bright spots outnumber the dark. Life is not all music in the minor—far less a clash of discord and dissonance. It is rather made up of blended harmonies.

. . . After he had served his own generation by the will of God, he fell on sleep . . . (Acts 13:36).

September 25th is ever kept in memory as the Coronation Day of the one known throughout the earth's bounds as Charles E. Cowman, Missionary Warrior. We treasure the memory. It is perfume sweet.

"I love better to count time from spring to spring. It seems to me far more cheerful to count the years by blossom than by blight" were favorite lines found beautifully penned between the leaves of his well-worn Bible.

I shall meet him when my earthly task is finished and my morning dawns. *L. B. C.*

God's people never meet for the last time.

For now we see through a glass darkly; but then face to face: now I know in part; but then shall I know even as also I am known (1 Cor. 13:12).

Death is called the key that opens the palace of eternity. Tennyson thinking of Hallam, his friend, who had been drowned at sea, calls him "That friend of mine who lives in God."

Drummond suggests that death is not so much "sunset" as "sunrise"; not so much "departure" as "arrival." Dying Frances Willard exclaimed, "How beautiful it is to be with God!"

For the Christian, one declares that "to be death-called is to be God-called, to be God-called is to be Christ-found, and to be Christ-found is hope, home and heaven."

Morn shall break and I will stand at daybreak in my Fatherland. The western gates close to let the Eastern gates open.

> From the dust of the weary highway,
>   From the smart of sorrow's rod,
> Into the royal Presence,
>   They are bidden as guests or God.
> The veil from their eyes is taken,
>   Sweet mysteries they are shown,
> Their doubts and fears are over,
>   For they know as they are known.
>
> For them there should be rejoicing
>   For them the festal array,
> As for the bride in her beauty,
>   Whom love hath taken away;
> Sweet hours of peaceful waiting
>   Till the path that we have trod,
> Shall end at the Father's gateway,
>   And we are the guests of God.

In his dying hour Charles Kingsley was heard to whisper, "How beautiful God is."

For thou wilt light my candle . . . (Psalm 18:28).

In a dimly-lighted room a girl was found working with unwonted haste. When asked the reason, she replied, "My candle is nearly burned out and I don't have another."

Robert Louis Stevenson, in speaking of a friend said, "When he comes into a room it is as though someone had lighted another candle."

An enlightened soul is like a lighted candle. One candle can light a thousand others without diminishing its light.

The beauty of a candle touches me—it is so softly gay, so steadfast and so careless of itself—giving itself away.

> To give of self, and not to count the cost,
> To learn, to teach, to labor and to pray,
> To serve like Christ, the least, the last, the lost—
> These were the beacon fires that lit the way.

*And, mind you, I am alongside you all the days . . . (Matt. 28:20—
Berkeley Version).*

> Lonely? Yes, sometimes when the night is dark
>   And silence wraps the spirit in its gloom;
> But then his angels, watching ever nigh,
>   Supply the place of friendship's room.
>
> Tired? Yes, often when the day is done,
>   And sun rays sink behind the distant west;
> But then my Saviour walks beside; and He
>   Can give the wearied heart its rest.
>
> Afraid? Oh yes, when mountain paths are steep,
>   Too steep for feet unused to rugged ways;
> But then His promise cheers me, and the fear
>   Is turned to joyful hymns of praise.
>
> So on I press, the loneliness and fear
>   But bind me closer to the love divine;
> Within the deepest darkness faith can see;
>   And so I pray: "Thy will, not mine."   *R. Hare.*

Closer is He than breathing; nearer than hands and feet.

Thou shalt guide me with thy counsel . . . (Psalm 73:24).

There are numberless things before us continually in our earthly pilgrimage regarding which we need counsel, we need advice; and when under these circumstances we should go to our Lord Jesus Christ and say to Him: "My Lord, I am ignorant; now what am I to do? Thou are my Counselor, now show me clearly and distinctly how to act under these circumstances." And what will be the result? You will be taught.

You need never take a step in the dark. If you do, you are sure to make a mistake. Wait until you have light. Remind the Lord Jesus that as He is Counselor to the Church of God, that He will be in your particular case Counselor and Guide and will direct you. If you patiently wait, believingly, expectantly wait, you will find that the waiting is not in vain and that the Lord will prove Himself a Counselor both wise and good.

Place the reins in His hands.

. . . Be thou faithful unto death, and I will give thee a crown of life (Rev. 2:10).

It may never be mine,
  In the noon-tide of day
With the victors to walk the proud street;
  My name may not shine
In the triumph so gay;
  Not for me would the laurel be meet.

With no bugles' loud blare,
  And no ringing of bell,
And no banner afloat on the breeze;
  No loud paen rare,
On the live air to swell,
  Little merit have I to hear these.

No noon-tide of glory,
  Nor melodious song,
Just a grave, and above me but sod;
  No theme for story,
And no fame to prolong;
  I just fought in the gloaming with God.

Dr. W. B. Hinson.

Let us be content to do but little if God sets us at little tasks. It is but pride and self-will which says, "Give me something huge to fight and I should enjoy that; but why make me sweep the dust?"

Charles Kingsley.

But his delight is in the law of the Lord, and in his law doth he meditate day and night (Psalm 1:2).

The passing of Edwin Markham has unusual interest for the Christian world. This great poet was devoted to God's Word, and was a daily reader of STREAMS IN THE DESERT. His poem, "Defeat May Serve As Well As Victory," is found under January 18 in this book.

A man of large physique, at the ripe age of eighty-four he seemed to possess the physical energy of a man much younger. He was in complete command of his marvelous mental faculties. It was an inspiration to hear the firm way in which he expressed his convictions. He told a group of friends that as a young man he had "steeped himself in the Gospels." For many years he could recite all of Matthew's Gospel from memory, and this was the Book that inspired the poem which won him world fame.

Speaking to a group of school teachers, he said of the Parables of Jesus, *"Of all the world's religious literature, these are its crowning glory."* He was a lifelong worker in the cause of human justice, and all this interest in mankind came from his love for Matthew's Gospel.

A merry heart doeth good like a medicine . . . (Prov. 17:22).

The secret of happy days is not in our outward circumstances, but in our own heart life. A large draught of Bible taken every morning, a throwing open of the soul's windows to the precious promises of the Lord, a season of fervent prayer, a deed or two of kindness to the people you meet, will brighten your countenance, and make your feet "like hind's feet" for the day's march. If you want to get your aches and your trials out of sight, bury them under your mercies. Begin every day with God, and then keeping step with your Lord, march on toward Home over the roughest road, or in the face of the hardest wind that blows. Live for Jesus by the day, and every day, until you come to the city where "the Lamb is the light thereof," and there is no night.

One courageous thought will put to flight a host of troubles.

_____

The path of the just is as the shining light that shineth more and more unto the perfect day (Prov. 4:18).

The cynical poet says, "Old age is dark." The Christian's life refutes the calumny. The brightest bars of gold, set in the sky are at twilight. The last beams of day are the golden ones.

> For while the tired waves, vainly breaking
>   Seem here no painful inch to gain,
> Far back, through creeks and inlets making
>   Comes silent, flooding in, the main.
>
> And not by eastern windows only,
>   When daylight comes, comes in the light;
> In front the sun climbs slow—how slowly—
>   But westward look, the land is bright.   *A. H. Clough.*

. . . I know whom I have believed, and am persuaded that he is able to keep that which I have committed unto him . . . (2 Tim. 1:12).

A dear Christian once said to me: "I have always known that He is called the good Shepherd, but it meant nothing to me; and I believe I read the twenty-third Psalm as though it were written, 'The Lord is the sheep, and I am the shepherd, and if I don't keep a tight hold on Him, He will run away.'

"When dark days came, I never thought that He would stick by me; and when my soul was starving and cried out for food, I never dreamed He would feed me. I see now that I never looked upon Him as a faithful Shepherd at all.

"I myself am not one bit better or stronger, but I have discovered I have a good Shepherd and that is all I need! I see now it really is true that 'the Lord is my Shepherd, and I shall not want.' " *Mrs. Pearsall Smith.*

When we realize that God gives His attention to us personally, then we understand the sweetness of the words "My Shepherd."

God makes special study of the necessities of his children.

God is a shelter and a stronghold for us, we shall find Him very near, therefore we never fear . . . (Psalm 46:1-2—Moffatt Trans.).

Just think of that odd little sparrow,
　Uncared for by any but God,
It surely must bring thee some comfort
　To know that He loved it—though odd.

That one little odd little sparrow,
　The object of God's tender care?
Then surely thou art of more value,
　Thou need'st not give way to despair.

It may be thou art an "odd sparrow,"
　But God's eye of love rests on thee,
And he understands what to others,
　Will always a mystery be.

Thou thinkest thy case so peculiar
　That nobody can understand.
Take life's tangled skein to Thy Saviour
　And leave it in His skillful Hand.

Believe in His love and His pity
　Confide in his wisdom and care,
Remember the little odd sparrow,
　And never give way to despair.

Never through eternity can harm befall God's own children, in His Home.

Whosoever liveth and believeth in me shall never die . . . (John 11:26).

S peaking from the pulpit a year after the commencement of the disease from which he ultimately died, Dr. W. B. Hinson said, "I remember a year ago when a man in this city said, 'You have got to go to your death.' I walked out to where I live, five miles out of this city, and I looked across that mountain that I love, and I looked at the river in which I rejoice, and I looked at the stately trees that are always God's own poetry to my soul. Then in the evening I looked up into the great sky where God was lighting His lamps, and I said, 'I may not see you many more times, but mountain, I shall be alive when you are gone; and river, I shall be alive when you cease running toward the sea; and stars, I shall be alive when you have fallen from your sockets in the great down-pulling of the Universe.' "

Faith and hope must rise, plume their wings and soar toward the sunrise clouds of gold.

. . . This is the victory that overcometh the world, even our faith (1 John 5:4).

O Lord, as old age overtakes me, save me from two evils, on the one hand, the querulous, critical, fault-finding habits into which so many old people fall; and on the other, the soft, gullible spirit. Keep my eyes wide open to this weakness, foolishness, guilefulness, and sin of men; yet keep my heart tender, sympathetic and hopeful.

Help me to be firm and steadfast in my loyalty to truth and always clear as to what the truth is. Don't let me be deceived. Don't let me go astray the very least in my old age.

Don't permit me to fall even into a little folly, which like the fly in the pot of ointment, will spoil the influence of a life devoted to Thee. *Samuel Brengle.*

At evening time there shall be light—not an unusually bright twilight, but a fresh sunrise.

And now behold, the Lord hath kept me alive, as he said, these forty and five years . . . while the children of Israel wandered in the wilderness: and now, lo, I am this day fourscore and five years old. As yet I am as strong this day as I was in the day that Moses sent me: as my strength was then, even so is my strength now, for war, both to go out and to come in (Josh. 14:10, 11).

G od dealt justly and liberally with this old saint. . . . At the age of eighty-five he met the challenge of the hardest task of his life! Forty years of wilderness life had not dimmed his vision, lessened his faith, dulled his youthful zeal, nor diminished his physical powers. This is the heritage of those who wholly follow the Lord . . . Old age is no bar to the power of God.

Dr. McConnell built a great church in the city of Atlanta at the age of seventy. J. Hudson Taylor at seventy was vigorously pushing into new territory, opening new fields to the Gospel and praying out new bands of missionaries to Inland China. George Mueller at ninety was still expanding and enlarging a work that not only housed 1,500 orphans, but was publishing religious literature and sending out missionaries to half a dozen mission fields. So, in his old age, Caleb went up to the stronghold of the Anakim, and dislodged them from their fortress and took possession of their cities.

"Let us go up at once . . . for we are well able to overcome it," is the victorious cry of a triumphant faith and its reward is to reign in the place it has wrested from the hand of its fiercest enemies.

Do not fret therefore in view of tomorrow for tomorrow will have its own anxieties (Matt. 6:34—Berkeley Version).

You and I are to take our trials, our black Fridays, our lone and long nights, and we are to come to Him and say, "Manage these, Thou Wondrous Friend, Who canst turn the very night into the morning; manage these for me!"

> I heard a voice at evening softly say,
>   Bear not thy yesterday into tomorrow;
> Nor load this week with last week's load of sorrow.
>   Lift all thy burdens as they come, nor try
> To weight the present with the by and by.
>   One step and then another, take thy ways—
>   Live by the day!
>
> Though autumn leaves are withering round thy way,
>   Walk in the sunshine. It is all for thee.
> Push straight ahead, as long as thou canst see.
>   Dread not the winter whither thou mayst go,
> But when it comes, be thankful for the snow.
>   Onward and upward, look and smile and pray—
>   Live by the day!   *J. H. May.*

Today is the tomorrow you worried about yesterday.

For the Lord is a great God . . . He is our God . . . (Psalm 95:3, 7).

In 1897, one year before Mr. Mueller died (in his ninety-third year), he wrote, "I have been a lover of the Word of God for sixty-eight years and three months—and that uninterruptedly. During this time I have read considerably more than one hundred times through the whole of the Old and New Testaments with prayer and meditation.

"My great love for the Word of God and my deep conviction of the need of its being spread far and wide, have led me to pray to God to use me as an instrument to do this, and to supply me with means for it; and He has condescended to enable me to circulate the Scriptures in all parts of the earth, and in various languages; and has been pleased thus simply through the reading of the Scriptures to bring thousands of precious souls to the knowledge of the Lord Jesus."

Through prayer and faith, Mr. Mueller provided and cared for 10,000 orphans at Ashley Down, Bristol, England.

God cause us to be conservative in our faith and radical in its application.

But if we hope for that we see not, then do we with patience wait for it (Rom. 8:25).

S ometimes when the horizon is all cloud-banked and the lightnings are leaping and the dismal thunder growls, I say, "Never mind, soon the storm will be over and I shall see God's city." Sometimes when every joy seems to die and every staff breaks under my head, I say, "Never mind, a few more sunsets and I shall see God's city, the city that hath foundations, whose maker and builder is God."

It will be a wonderful place. No one ever sheds a tear there, no one is sick, the hands never shake, the feet never drag, the eyelid never droops, for they are healthy forever in that city. They do not need stars at night because they have no night; and they do not need a sun by day, because they have no days; but the smile on the face of God is the Eternal, never-dimmed light in which the glorified walk and exult in the city of God.

I am bound for the beautiful City!

> Lord Jesus Thou didst still the angry sea,
> This trembling hand thou canst, oh, still for me.
> I know Thou wilt, if I believe in Thee,
> Someday make still this trembling hand for me.

I was dumb, I opened not my mouth; because thou didst it (Psalm 39:9).

It is said that sometimes gardeners, when they would bring a rose to richer flowerings, deprive it for the season of light and moisture. Silent and dark it stands, dropping one fading leaf after another, and seeming to go down patiently to death.

But, when every leaf is dropped, and the plant stands stripped to the uttermost, a new life is even then working in the buds, from which will spring a tender foliage and a brighter wealth of flowers; so often in celestial gardenings, every leaf of earthly joy must drop before a new and divine bloom visits the soul.

> Love looked down with eyes so tender
> All the room was wrapt in gloom,
> And I deemed him but a stranger,
> Knowing naught of my sad doom—
> "Who art thou?" I whispered, breathless.
> "Child," Love said, "this is our tryst.
> Only thus could'st thou have met me
> In such sweetness . . . I am Christ."

When God is going to do something wonderful, He begins with a difficulty. If He is going to do something very wonderful, He begins with an impossibility.

Whoso is wise, and will observe these things, even they shall understand the loving kindness of the Lord (Psalm 107:43).

On a low branch in the woods up the river, I found a cocoon. Such a gray, drab little thing, I thought as I rested on a rock near it. But there was life shut up in that dark bit of unpromising shell—that would soon emerge with shining colorful wings. Not all at once. The little creature would hang tremulously at first to the branch and move its wings slowly up and down until they took on form and beauty.

Cocoon experiences are not limited to those little creatures, I mused, flipping a pebble into the water. But deep in the heart of life's grayest days, God is preparing wings and delicate beauty and strength. Moses spent his cocoon days in the wilderness, but he emerged after forty years with strength to accomplish a great work for God. Wrapped in the gloom of sorrow, trial, perplexity, we may spend wintry days, but the spring will come when the purpose of those days will manifest itself as slowly as the cocoon breaks about us and we come out again into sunlit days, changed, but more glorious than when we went in.

The thickest clouds bring the heaviest shower of blessing.

The path of the righteous is as the light of dawn, going on and brightening unto meridian day (Prov. 4:18—Rotherham).

Doubtless you have seen a creeper growing up a high house wall. At the top was a wealth of flowers and leaves, spreading wider the higher it went, but downwards, it all narrowed to a bare, wrinkled, single stem, so touched by the passing seasons that but for the life above it, you would say it is dead.

Can you believe that God gave any man the gift of life, meaning the first half to be the best? What God begins He completes. God will finish what He has begun. If you will keep the incense burning there—His glory you shall see, sometime, somewhere.

> Our times are in His hand
> Who saith "A whole I planned;
> Youth shows but half; trust God;
> See all, nor be afraid."

The thing to do is neither to fear old age nor to fight it, but accept it without tension and use it. Don't bear old age, nor accommodate yourself to it, but take hold of this stage of life and make something beautiful out of it.

. . . His compassions fail not. They are new every morning; great is thy faithfulness (Lam. 3:22, 23).

There are some people who have a pitiful dread of old age. For myself, instead of its being a matter of sorrow or of pain, it is rather an occasion of profound joy that God has enabled me to write in my family record, "four score years."

The October of life may be one of the most fruitful months in all its calendar; and the Indian summer its brightest period when God's sunshine kindles every leaf on the tree with crimson and golden glories. Faith grows in its tenacity of fiber by the long continued exercise of testing God, and trusting His promises. The veteran Christian can turn over the leaves of his well-worn Bible and say, "This Book has been my daily companion; I know all about this promise and that one and that other one, for I have tried them for myself. I have a great pile of checks which my Heavenly Father has cashed with gracious blessings."

Bunyan brings his pilgrim, not into a second infant school where they may sit down in imbecility, or loiter in idleness; be brings them into Beulah Land where the birds fill the air with music; and where they catch glimpses of the Celestial City. They are drawing nearer the end of their journey and beyond that river—that has no bridge—looms up the New Jerusalem in all its flashing splendors. *Theodore L. Cuyler.*

Old age can be looked forward to with anticipation and a sense of adventure.

With long life will I satisfy him, and show him my salvation (Psalm 91:16).

> Ah nothing is too late till the tired heart shall cease
>   to palpitate.
> Cato learned Greek at eighty; Sophocles wrote his grand
>   *Oedipus* and Simonides
> Bore off the prize of verse from his compeers
> When each had numbered more than fourscore years.
>
> Chaucer, at Woodstock with the nightingales,
> At sixty wrote the *Canterbury Tales;*
> Goethe at Weimar, toiling to the last
> Completed *Faust* when eighty years were past.
>
> For age is opportunity no less
> Than youth itself, though in another dress,
> And as the evening twilight fades away
> The sky is filled with stars, invisible by day.
>
> *Henry W. Longfellow.*

Old age need not be a period of fainting. You can go down with your real powers unabated as you "walk" from one life to another.

And their eyes were opened, and they knew him . . . (Luke 24:31).

In 1875 a young Christian, whose testimony to his faith in Christ had been met by the rejoinder that it was only phantom and sham, prayed in a meeting definitely asking the Lord that Frances Ridley Havergal might write a poem "to show what Thou art—a living bright Reality"; and waxing bold, he added, "and let her do it this very night."

On that evening Miss Havergal was at another meeting where a man in his prayer used the expression: "Father, we know the reality of Jesus Christ." The expression made such a deep impression upon her that she went home and wrote a poem of nine stanzas, and dated it. When she recounted the incident, she added, "Does not this show the reality of prayer?"

> Reality, reality, Lord Jesus Christ Thou art to me;
> From the spectral mists and driving clouds,
> From the shifting shadows and phantom crowds,
> I turn to my glorious rest in Thee,
> Who art the grand reality.

We are not left to the dim stars or to the flicker of the uncertain lanterns. God Himself has spoken to us in the words of Jesus Christ.

Cause me to hear thy lovingkindness in the morning; for in thee do I trust: cause me to know the way wherein I should walk; for I lift up my soul unto thee (Psalm 143:8).

Morning! The air is fresh; the birds sing at their best. It is a new birth of time. Sameness is relieved, abolished; this is another day. "In the morning will I direct my prayer unto thee." Surely this is the voice in melody. It is the voice in song and also in prayer with the upward look.

But, how early? Rather, how soon after awaking should praise and prayer begin? If there can be nothing in sleep to disturb God's care of us and love for us, shall we, who are the recipients of His marvelous grace, allow Satan to steal the first waking moments and fill them with fears, murmurs, groans and sighs, allowing praise and prayer to be deferred until after this robbery?

For what is sleep? If our Lord "giveth unto his beloved in sleep" (Psalm 127:2, RV, margin), then sleep is a time of special receiving from Him. It is the opposite to worry, struggle and murmur. It is the time when He carries us, as it were, in His safe-keeping over to the very verge of eternity, and after refreshing us there, lo, when we awake He has brought us back to a new world, a new day—a fresh-born, a God-made day. Who then watched and cared? Why, when we were unconscious, He brought us safely to this symbolized resurrection. Who? Who did it? Who but our Lord. Shall we then allow Satan to steal these first waking moments at the peep of day whether we awaken early or late?

Lord, claim my every day, my every hour—and this one at the peep o' day.

And when he had sent the multitudes away, he went up into a mountain apart to pray; and when the evening was come, he was there alone (Matt. 14:23).

Haydn once was in company of other noted artists when one of them asked how one might recover strength quickest after a period of great exertion.

Different methods were suggested, but when Haydn was asked what methods he followed, he said: "In my home I have a small chapel. When I feel wearied, because of my work, I go there and pray. This remedy has never failed me."

Experience tells us that Haydn was right. In believing prayer, we tap the source of all strength.

Madame Guyon wrote, "I love the lovely creative hours with God."

A calm hour with God is worth a whole lifetime with man.

Let everything that hath breath praise the Lord . . . (Psalm 150:6).

Wʜᴀᴛ a joy it is to have a singing heart! And if you are not singing your thanks and joy, He is missing it. Earth's oratorio is not complete to Him without your note of thanksgiving.

> Thou who hast given so much to me,
> Give one thing more—a grateful heart;
> Not thankful when it pleaseth me,
> As if thy blessings had spare days,
> But such a heart, whose pulse may be
>   Thy praise!
>
> *George Herbert.*

The Lord does not impose a foreign joy trying to make us happy in something we cannot be happy in. Every joy, other than His, leaves us dissatisfied, incomplete.

But thanks be to God, which giveth us the victory through our Lord Jesus Christ (1 Cor. 15:57).

When I look back and read of the early Christians, I am charmed to find how they always felt about dying. They had such a sense of dying in Jesus, such a sense of the reality of the Heavenly Home, such a sense of the glory of the future state, that they could take their children, and put them, as it were, into the hands of God, and rejoice and sing hymns of gratulation that they were about to go; and they could meet together over their dead as men meet to celebrate a great victory. This feeling is lost out of the Church; it is largely lost out of men's apprehension; and it seems to me that it will be one of the beneficent features in the development of Christianity in our age, and in the future ages, to bring back again in the experience of men, the beauty of death, the triumph of death and the overhanging light and glory that ought to destroy that darkness which to us, for the most part, envelopes the door of the grave.

When we comprehend the fullness of what death will do for us, in all our outlook and in all our forelook, dying is triumphing. Not any bower of roses is so festooned in June. Not where the jessamine and honeysuckle twine, and lovers sit, is there so fair a sight, so sweet a prospect, as where a soul in its early years is flying away, out of life and out of time, through the gate of death—the rosy gate of death, the royal gate of death, the golden gate of death, the pearly gate of death.

Dying, what is it? To shut out the black night and join the fireside of your Father's Home.   Robert E. Selle.

302

They that wait upon the Lord shall renew their strength . . . they shall run and not be weary; they shall walk and not faint (Isa. 40:31).

When Henry Wadsworth Longfellow was well along in years, his head was white as snow, but his cheeks were as red as a rose. An ardent admirer asked him how it was that he was able to keep so vigorous and to write so beautifully.

Pointing to a blossoming apple tree nearby, the poet replied: "That apple tree is very old, but I never saw prettier blossoms upon it than those which it now bears. The tree grows a little new wood each year, and I suppose that it is out of the new wood that those blossoms come. Like the apple tree, I try to grow a little new wood each year."

> Age is the harvest, when all men must reap
> What they have sown; some bitterly must weep
> O'er wasted time; while some their sheaves will bind
> With hearts of joy and with a peaceful mind.
>
> Age is the Eventide, now work is done;
> The shadows lengthen, setting is the sun;
> The tasks were heavy, and the labor hard,
> But everlasting is the rich reward.

. . . I will fear no evil for thou art with me . . . (Psalm 23:4).

Little one, you must not fret,
  That I take your clothes away.
Better sleep you so will get
  And at morning wake more gay—
  Saith the children's mother.

You must I unclothe again,
  For you need a better dress,
Too much worn are body and brain,
  Saith the Heavenly Father.

I went down death's lovely stair;
  Laid my garments in the tomb;
Dressed again one morning fair;
  Hastened up and hied me home,
  Saith the Elder Brother.

Then I will not be afraid
  Any ill can come to me;
When 'tis time to go to bed,
  I will rise and go with Thee,
  Saith the little brother.
                              George MacDonald.

God delights to disappoint man's fears.

. . . Whatsoever a man soweth, that shall he also reap (Gal. 6:7).

How have you made out to live so long and be so well?" asked a young man of one who was ninety years of age. The old man took the younger to an orchard. Pointing to some large trees full of apples, he said, "I planted those trees when I was a boy, and do you wonder that now I am permitted to gather fruit of them?" "Whatsoever a man soweth that shall he also reap."

We gather in old age what we plant in youth. Plant in early life the right kind of Christian character, and you will eat the luscious fruit in old age and gather the harvest in eternity.

T. DeWitt Talmadge.

Why stay we on earth unless it be to grow?

Blessed is the man . . . (whose) delight is in the law of the Lord . . . He shall be like a tree planted by the rivers of water, that bringeth forth his fruit in his season; his leaf also shall not wither; and whatsoever he doeth shall prosper (Psalm 1:1-3).

I love a tree,
A brave, upstanding tree!
When I am wearied in the strife,
Beaten by storms and bruised by life,
I look up at a tree and it refreshes me.
If it can keep its head held high,
And look the storms straight in the eye,
Ready to stand, ready to die,
Then by the grace of God, can I—
At least with Heaven's help, I'll try;
I love a tree, for it refreshes me.

I love a tree.
When it seems dead,
Its leaves all shorn and bared its head,
When winter flings its cold and snow,
It stands there undismayed by woe;
It stands there waiting for the spring—
A tree is such a believing thing.
I love a tree,
For it refreshes me.   *Ralph Spaulding Cushman.*

The fullness of life does not come from the things outside of us: we ourselves must create the beauty in which we live.

. . . Ye shall find rest for your souls . . . (Jer. 6:16).

L aid aside by illness? No, laid aside for stillness.

I have found a great deal of comfort more than once in my own experience in a little word of the Shepherd Psalm—"He maketh me to lie down in green pastures." I like to emphasize the "maketh" for we are not always willing ourselves to stop for rest, and gentle compulsion is needed. He will not have me always on the stretch. The bow of the best violin sometimes needs to have its strings loosened, and so my Lord gives me rest.

Then it is pleasant to know that it is not on the dusty road, nor on the dreary, parched hillside, that we are made to lie down, but in the green pastures. It is only and always for rest and renewal that we are made to stop and lie down. The time is not lost.

Dr. J. R. Miller.

> And I smiled to think God's greatness flowed
>   Around our incompleteness!
> Round our restlessness—His rest!   *E. B. Browning.*

For here we have no continuing city, but we seek one to come (Heb. 13:14).

The words often on Jesus' lips in his last days express vividly the idea, "Going to the Father." We too, who are Christ's people, have vision of something beyond the difficulties and disappointments of this life. We are journeying toward fulfillment, completion, expansion of life. We, too, are "going to the Father." Much is dim concerning our home country, but two things are clear. It is home, "the Father's House." It is the nearer presence of the Lord. *We are all wayfarers, but the believer knows it and accepts it. He is a traveler, not a settler.*

> The little birds trust God, they go singing
>   From northern woods where autumn winds have blown,
> With joyous faith their trackless pathway winging
>   To summer lands of song, afar, unknown.
>
> Let us go singing, then, and not go sighing
>   Since we are sure our times are in His hand,
> Why should we weep, and fear, and call it dying?
>   'Tis only flitting to a Summer land.

While I was praying, the answer came, brought by the angel Gabriel, who was caused by the Lord to fly swiftly (Dan. 9:21—Modern Trans.).

It is said that in one of Spurgeon's prayer meetings, a little boy rose and asked prayer that his father might read the Bible. After prayer was offered Mr. Spurgeon looked for the boy and could not find him. At the conclusion of the meeting he saw the lad and asked him why he had left the meeting. He replied, "After you prayed for my father to read the Bible, I ran home to see him do it."

"Did he do it?" Mr. Spurgeon asked. "Yes, there he was reading it; and I came back to tell you."

> God makes a promise,
> Faith believes it,
> Hope anticipates it,
> Patience quietly awaits it.

. . . Who maketh the clouds His chariots (Psalm 104:3).

It is for us, therefore, to feel assured that the clouds of life, often so black, so gloomy, hiding the sunlight, are in reality the chariots of God.

Believe that your present trial is the thundercloud with a rainbow sleeping in its folds.

> Oh, make my clouds thy chariots,
>   So shall I learn to see
> That the mist that dims the glory
>   Is itself a light from Thee.
>
> For the shadow of the wilderness
>   To me shall sing aloud,
> When I find they nearest coming,
>   In the advent of a cloud.

The God who is better to you than all your fears, perhaps intends the affliction to remain with you until it lifts the latch of heaven and lets you into your eternal rest.

Ye shall have a song . . . (Isa. 30:29).

S omeone writes of sitting one winter evening by an open wood fire and listening to the singing of the green logs as the fire flamed about them. All manner of sounds came out of the wood as it burned, and the writer, with poetic fancy, suggests that they were imprisoned songs, long sleeping in silence in the wood, brought out now by the fire.

When the tree stood in the forest, the birds came and sat on its boughs and sang their songs. The wind, too, breathed through the branches, making a weird, strange music. One day a child sat on the moss by the tree's root and sang its happy gladness in a snatch of sweet melody. A penitent sat under the tree's shade and with trembling tones, amid falling leaves, sang the fifty-first Psalm. And all these notes of varied song sank into the tree as it stood there and hid away in its trunk. There they slept until the tree was cut down and part of it became a back-log in the cheerful fire. Then the flames brought out the music.

This is but a poet's fancy as far as the tree and the songs of the back-log are concerned. But, is there not here a little parable which may be likened to many a human life? Life has its varied notes and tones. *Remember, gather the driftwood, that will light the winter fire!*

. . . And God, even our own God, shall bless us (Psalm 67:6).

A party stood on the Matterhorn admiring the sumblimity of the scene, when a gentleman produced a pocket microscope, and having caught a fly, placed it under the glass. He reminded the rest of the party that the legs of the household fly in England are naked. He then called attention to the legs of this little fly which were thickly covered with hair—thus showing that the same God who made the lofty Swiss mountain attended to the comfort of His tiniest creatures, even providing socks and mittens for the little fly whose home these mountains were! This God is our God!

God is great in great things, but very great in little things!

. . . Whose leaf shall not fade . . . (Ezek. 47:12).

The pages of sacred and profane history are replete with instances wherein persons over sixty years of age have done their best work.

It is true as the Bible says: "We all do fade as a leaf" (Isa. 64:6); but what a difference in the fading of leaves.

Some leaves wither brownly like the alder and the butternut. Some put on golden hues like the white birch and the quaking aspen.

Some are arrayed in glad colors of scarlet and yellow like the red oak and the maple.

Who, with the least bit of love of nature in his constitution, has not taken time out and even gone out of his way to see the hills crowned and the vales filled with the glory and the splendor of fading leaves!

Is it not true that certain trees renew in their autumn foliage the same color that marked them in the budding time of spring, but with deeper, fuller hues?

It is the spirit of old age that determines whether it be a nightmare or a golden sunset.

_____

Turn you to the stronghold, ye prisoners of hope . . . (Zech. 9:12).

God is waiting to prove Himself to us a God of deliverance. Never think for one moment that He means to keep you in prison. That is not His purpose. Those who so far misunderstood Him pray only for strength, courage, and patience to endure. God does answer those prayers; yet He would far rather see His children go a step beyond and pray for deliverance, freedom and triumph.

Do you think that it is His will to see us sad, crushed and sorrowing all our days? Do you think that we could best glorify Him so?

Let us be "prisoners of hope"—looking for the opening of the door—for the breaking of our chains. Then, soon, we shall be able to pass out through the open door, to glorify Him in freedom and joy, for the great work by which He has caused us to triumph over our sorrows.

As an advocate, He never loses a case. He will never lose our case for He pleads effectively.

Thou shalt know also that thy seed shall be great, and thine offspring as the grass of the earth (Job 5:25).

When the sun goes below the horizon, it is not set; the heavens glow for a full hour after its departure. And when a great and good man "sets," the sky of this world is luminous long after he is out of sight. Such a man cannot die out of this world. When he goes, he leaves behind him much of himself.

This should be at once the crown of all our hopes for the future, and the one great lesson taught us by the vicissitudes of life. The joys and sorrows, the journeying and the rest, the temporary repose and the frequent struggles; all these should make us sure that there is an end which will interpret them all, to which they all point, for which they all prepare.

> Winging my way
> Into the sun-flecked dawn,
> If I should not return,
> Say not, I'm gone.
>
> If what I lived for
> Still lives on
> In younger hearts,
> It still is Dawn.

Dr. B. H. Pearson.

And deliver those who through fear of death were all their lifetime subject to bondage (Heb. 2:15).

John Wesley said, "Brethren, farewell. The greatest thing is that God still lives. Brethren, farewell,"

John Wesley stepped into his chariot and he rode on. That is the Christian way. When Moody was leaving this world for the other, he said to his wife, "Do you hear that singing?" Then he said, "Earth is receding, Heaven is opening," and he was gone.

That is beautiful. That is the Christian way to go. That is the glory of the death moment. Still *we live foolishlu our whole life afraid of death.*

> As sings the mountain stream
>   Past rock and verdure wild.
> So let me sing my way to Thee,
>   Thy pure and happy child.

When his candle shined upon my head, and when by his light I walked through darkness (Job 29:3).

The artist needs the gray days in order to know fully the beauty of the world in which he lives. If the hidden sun and the clouded sky dissuade him from wandering abroad, he will lose much that is worth his observation.

Thank God for life's gray days, as well as for His sunshine. How should we know the beauty of local color in the characters of our friends and loved ones, if we saw them always and only when the sun is shining, when its golden rays of prosperity, health and abundant happiness falls upon them?

It is in the gray days that we discover unsuspected wonder of patience, courage and unselfishness; then we discover that beneath the gilding of good fortune there was a form of strength and beauty, that submerged by the glare of fame or wealth or popularity, there were values of personality which now stand forth as never before.

Thank God for life's gray days—not merely, as is often said, because they heighten our appreciation of the sunshine, but because in themselves they have a realm of charm as wonderful, as heartening, as appealing as any which the sun in all its magnificence of blazing light reveals.

> Just as the year has its June and December
> Snow wreaths in winter and blossoms in May;
> Sunshine in summer and fogs in November,
> 'Tis always the darkest the hour before day.

*. . . He shall gather the lambs with his arm, and carry them in his bosom
. . . (Isa. 40:11).*

Come, my sheep
Shadows deep
Fall o'er land and sea.
Fast the day
Fades away,
Come and rest with me.
Come, and in my fold abide,
Dangers lurk on every side
Till at last
Night has passed
In my fold abide.

Come my sheep
I will keep
Watch, the long night through.
Safe from harm
And alarm
I will shelter you.
Through the night, my lambs shall rest
Safe upon their Shepherd's breast.
Folded there,
Free from care,
Through the night, shall rest.

Come my sheep,
Calmly sleep
Sheltered in the fold.
Weary one,
Homeward come,
Winds are blowing cold.
Rest until the dawn shall break,
Then with joy my flocks shall wake.
Pastures new
Wait for you
When the dawn shall break.   *Dorothy B. Polsue.*

*The Lord is thy keeper—but not thy jailer. His keeping is not
confinement, it is protection. When you commit your ways to Him,
He does not abridge your liberty; He only defends you against the
evil.*

I will satiate the soul of the priests with fatness, and my people shall be satisfied with my goodness, saith the Lord (Jer. 31:14).

Christ is my Saviour. He is my life. He is everything to me in Heaven and earth. Once, while traveling in a sandy region, I was tired and thirsty. Standing on the top of a mound, I looked for water. The sight of a lake at the distance brought joy to me, for now I hoped to quench my thirst. I walked toward it for a long time, but I could never reach it. Afterward I found out that it was a mirage, only a mere appearance of water caused by the refracted rays of the sun. In reality there was none.

In a like manner, I was moving about the earth in search of the Water of Life. The things of this world—wealth, position, honour and luxury—looked like a lake by drinking of whose waters I hoped to quench my spiritual thirst. But I could never find a drop of water to quench the thirst of my heart. I was dying of thirst. When my spiritual eyes were opened, I saw the rivers of Living Waters flowing from His pierced side. I drank of it and was satisfied. Thirst was no more. Ever since I have always drunk of that Water of Life, and have never been athirst in the sandy desert of the world. My heart is full of praise.

His presence gives me a peace which passes all understanding, no matter in what circumstances I am placed. Amidst persecution I have found peace, joy and happiness. Nothing can take away the joy I have found in my Saviour. In home He was there. In prison He was there. In Him the prison was transformed into Heaven, and the Cross into a source of blessing.

Now, I have no desire for wealth, position and honor. Nor do I desire even Heaven. But I need Him who has made my heart heaven. His infinite love has expelled the love of all other things. The heart is the throne of the King of Kings. *The capital of Heaven is the heart where that King reigns.*   Sadhu Sundar Singh.

Better is the end of a thing than the beginning thereof . . . (Eccl. 7:8).

Farther on, you will find no thorns, but in every step you will tread out the fragrance of the sweetest flowers. Farther on you will meet with no foe; but kindred spirits with their great thoughts, wise and loving, will cheer you on the way. Farther on no dark cloud will throw its gloomy shadows over you; you shall have the brightest stars at night, and nought but sunshine in the day. Farther on, the prospect improves; the valleys are more rich and the mountains more grand; flowers of lovelier hue and sweeter fragrance are there; trees of statelier mould deck the landscape; and rivers and lakes more transparent and more majestic refresh and beautify the scene. Take courage, it is better farther on.

> I hear it singing, sweetly,
>   Softly in an undertone,
> Singing as if God had taught it—
>   It is better farther on!
>
> Night and day it sings the same song,
>   Sings it while I sit alone,
> Sings it that the heart may hear it—
>   It is better farther on.

. . . I am like a green fir tree . . . (Hosea 14:8).

B e you young until you die, as far as energy, persistence, ambition, and augmentation of resources are concerned. There are some things that curl over easily in autumn. Their leaves become sere and yellow and fall to the ground before there are any signs of frost in the air. I do not like such vegetables; I do not have them in my garden. Others carry their green leaves clean down into freezing before they give up. These I like. And I like to see men who can look at God's frosts and not be blighted, but remain green and succulent and growing, even into the edges of winter.   *Dr. Beecher.*

God blessed old age like the autumn leaves so that it brightens a gray day with the colors of the departed sun.

Try putting off old age to some other day.

. . . Be thou an example of the believer . . . (1 Tim. 4:12).

T he rest of the hillside was barren and gray. A light covering of snow lay over the grass and the sky overhead was dark and lowering. All the trees had dropped their leaves and stood gaunt against the horizon—all, that is, except one splendid pine.

There it stood in the midst of the wintry scene as green and as gay as it had been last summer. Something in its nature enabled it to survive the cold and maintain its beauty.

As we looked out the window, my traveling companion, motioning toward the noble tree, said, "I would like to think that my religion enabled me to survive the winter as that pine does. I would like to be a bright spot on the horizon, when everything else has gone into eclipse."

That is exactly what good religion ought to do for one. A cheerless, hopeless, worried, despairing Christian is an anomaly, a contradiction, and a denial of our Lord's power to redeem life for us.   *Roy L. Smith.*

_____

A bruised reed will he not break . . . (Matt. 12:20).

A fter he found himself no longer able to render active Christian service, Austin Phelps wrote, "One thought has assumed a new reality in my mind of late, as an offshoot of my useless life. When a man can do nothing else, he can add his little rill to the great river of intercessory prayer which is always rolling up to the throne of God. The river is made up of such rills as the ocean is of drops. A praying man can never be a useless man."

> Make use of me, my God!
>   Let me not be forgot;
> A broken vessel cast aside,
>   One whom Thou needest not.
>
> All things do serve Thee here,
>   All creatures, great and small;
> Make use of me, of me, My God—
>   The meanest of them all.   *Dr. Horatius Bonar.*

When a man enlists with God, he lets Him choose his rank and uniform.

. . . Unto Him that loved us, and washed us from our sins in His own blood, and hath made us kings and priests unto God and his Father; to him be glory and dominion forever and ever (Rev. 1:5, 6).

Who are those that dwell in Heaven forever and ever? Sinners saved by grace! There is not a man or woman there who was not a sinner.

I stand upon the golden streets, I walk amid the brightness of the city; I hear a man singing, and I say to him, "And what were you on earth?" He answers, "I am the thief who died by the side of Christ. I said, 'Lord remember me when Thou comest into Thy kingdom,' and He said, 'This day shalt thou be with me in Paradise,' and I have been here ever since."

I pass on and I say to another, "Who are you with the light upon your brow?" She answers: "I am the one who broke the alabaster box of ointment over the Saviour's feet; I washed his feet with tears and wiped them with the hairs of my head; and now He has wiped all my tears and I am happy in His presence."

"And who are you so radiant with happiness?" To which I receive the reply, "I am the man who had ten legions of devils; Jesus cast them out and healed me; and now I am praising Him forever."

Yes, these are the inhabitants of this Glorious city. It may be that when we get to glory and stand amid the redeemed, worshipping, we shall hear one saying, pointing to Jesus, "Do you see those marks upon His blessed brow? Those scars? It was I who plaited the crown of thorns and pressed it on His brow."

But why should not these sinners be in glory? The Blood of Christ availed as much for them as for you and me. I should not be surprised, such is the amazing love of God, at seeing any of these in glory.

They will come from all parts—from north, south, east and west. The dark faces and the pale faces are alike now. We shall go in with uplifted foreheads, to wear the crown, with eager feet to tread those golden streets, with longing eyes to gaze upon the face of Christ, to worship God and the Lamb.

Ye are a chosen generation . . . that ye should show forth the praises of him who hath called you out of darkness into his marvelous light (1 Peter 2:9).

The teacher of a Sunday School class once asked a little girl, "My dear, can you tell me what is a saint?"

Instantly the child's mind reverted to a visit she had made with her parents to a great cathedral. The windows were adorned with marvelously executed pictures in stained glass of noble men and women of past ages who had lived, suffered and died in service to God and humanity. The summer sunlight streamed through spattered patches of gorgeous colors over the dim interior of the temple. The beautiful sight had made a lasting impression on the child's mind and recalling it, she replied, *"A saint is a person who lets the light of heaven shine through."* Has any theologian ever given a finer definition of saintliness than that?

And a man shall be as an hiding place from the wind, and a covert from the tempest; as rivers of water in a dry place, as the shadow of a great rock in a weary land (Isa. 32:2).

To the weary traveler in a hot, dry country there can be no greater comfort than the refreshing shade of a cool and towering rock. Our text suggests a long journey, with trying winds, a tempest, a dry parched land. It is the hot mid-afternoon. There are miles ahead to be covered. Perhaps even in our hurried days, we can at least imagine the slow plodding journey, on foot or by animal, through the hot, dry valleys in a rainless summer. Then the towering rock and its sheltering shade.

Quite naturally this came to tell of the protection of God. "The Lord is my rock and my fortress." How true it is that we need God's shelter along the journey of life. His shadow and shelter are close at hand. Then, strength, renewed, we can press on again with his help.

We must not count the shadow of the rock as the end of the journey. It should merely be a resting place, so that with renewed strength we may finish what we have begun.

Thou wilt keep him in perfect peace, whose mind is stayed on thee: because he trusteth in thee (Isa. 26:3).

I look not back—God knows the fruitless effort,
The wasted hours, the sinning and regrets;
I leave them all with Him that blots the record
And graciously forgives and then forgets.

I look not forward, God sees all the future,
The road that short or long, will lead me home;
And He will face with me its every trial,
And bear for me the burden that may come.

I look not around me—then would fears assail me,
So wild the tumult of life's restless sea;
So dark the world, so filled with war and evil,
So vain the hope of comfort and of ease.

I look not inward, that would make me wretched,
For I have naught on which to stay my trust;
Nothing I see but failures and shortcomings,
And weak endeavors crumbling into dust.

But I look up—up into the face of Jesus!
For there my heart can rest, my fears are stilled;
And there is joy, and love and light for darkness,
And perfect peace, and every hope fulfilled.

Miss J. H. Hunt.

When we look within we are depressed, when we look around we are impressed, but when we look at Jesus Christ we are blessed.

. . . Even so father; for it seemed good in thy sight (Luke 10:21).

One day Bramwell Booth went to his aged father and told him that the doctors said they could do not more for his eyes. "Do you mean that I am blind and must remain blind?"

"I fear it is so," said Bramwell.

"Shall I never see your face again?" asked the old man.

"No, probably not in this world."

The General moved out his hand until he felt and clasped the hand of his son. "God must know best. Bramwell, I have done what I could for God and the people with my eyes. Now I shall do what I can for God and the people without my eyes."

Physical handicaps are often a blessing. Edison could have had his hearing restored by an operation. However, he refused; he said his deafness shut out noises and a lot of nonsense and enabled him to concentrate better on his work. Alfred Adler, psychologist, maintains that nearly all civilization is the outcome of efforts to overcome feelings of inferiority, often caused by physical weakness.

"It must be that when the Lord took from me one faculty, He gave me another; which is in no way impossible. I think of the beautiful Italian proverb: 'When God shuts a door, He opens a window.' "   *Helen Keller.*

. . . And many others, which ministered unto him of their substance (Luke 8:3).

There is a legend which says that long ago there dwelt in a royal palace three fair maids. While they were in the wonderful garden one morning, with its strong streams and blushing roses, there arose the question as to which of them had the most beautiful hands. Eleanor who had tinted her white fingers while gathering luscious strawberries, thought hers the most beautiful. Antoinette had been among the fragrant roses and her hands had partaken of their dewy sweetness. To her they were the loveliest, Joan had dipped her dainty fingers in the lucid stream and as the clear diamond drops sparkled on her tapered fingers she thought her hands the most beautiful.

Just then there came a beggar girl who asked for alms, but the royal maidens drew aside their rich robes and turned away. The beggar passed to a cottage nearby and a woman with sun-burned face and toil-stained hands gave her bread. The beggar, so the legend runs, was immediately transformed into an angel and appeared at the garden gate, saying, *"The most beautiful hands are those which are found ready to bless and help their fellowmen."*

. . . He showed them his hands . . . (Luke 24:40).

The following passage from *The Lady of the Chimney Corner* shows God's use of hands: "No, dear, but God takes a hand wherever He can find it and jist diz what He likes wi' it. Sometimes He takes a bishop's and lays it on a child's head in benediction; then He takes the han' of a docther t' relieve pain, th' han' of a mother t' guide her chile, an' sometimes He takes th' han' of an aul craither like me t' give a bit comfort to a neighbor. But they're all han's touched be His Spirit, an' His spirit is everywhere lukin' for han's to use."

God give us the hands ever ready and responsive for whatever His will may be.

> Take my hands and let them move,
> At the impulse of Thy love.

The hands that can do no brilliant thing for God may yet become hands of benediction to the world.

Whosoever shall give you a cup of water to drink in my name, because ye belong to Christ, verily I say unto you, he shall not lose his reward (Mark 9:41).

Frances Ridley Havergal, whose songs have been a benediction to mankind wrote of the power of little things.

> For the memory of a kindly word
> For long gone by,
> The fragrance of a fading flower
> Sent lovingly.
>
> The warm pressure of the hand,
> The tone of cheer,
> The note that only bears a verse
> From God's own Word.
> Such tiny things we hardly count
> As ministry.
> But when the heart is over-wrought
> Oh, who can tell
> The power of such tiny things
> To make it well.

There is nothing small that ministers to the happiness of a single soul.

There failed not ought of any good thing which the Lord had spoken . . . all came to pass (Josh. 21:45).

S ome day, even you—trembling, faltering one—shall stand upon the heights of glory, and look back upon all you have passed through, all you have narrowly escaped, all the perils through which He guarded you, and the sins from which He saved you; and you shall shout, with a meaning you cannot understand now, "Salvation unto Him Who sitteth upon the throne, and unto the Lamb."

Some day, He will sit down with us in that glorious home, and we shall have all the ages in which to understand the story of our lives. And He will read over again this old marked Bible with us. He will show us how He kept all these promises; He will explain to us the mysteries that we could not understand; He will recall to our memory the things we have long forgotten; He will go over again with us the Book of Life; He will recall all the finished story; and I am sure we will often cry: "Blessed Christ! You have been so true; you have been so good! Was there ever love like this!" And then the great chorus will be repeated once more—"There failed not ought of any good thing that He hath spoken; all came to pass."

Beloved, will you take these old promises afresh? Will you make an edition of your Bible not printed by the Bible Society, nor the Oxford Press, but a Bible written by the Holy Spirit upon your heart, and translated into the version of your life? And, some day, He will let us write upon its last page, this glorious inscription, "There failed not ought of any good thing which He spoke unto the House of Israel; all came to pass." *A. B. Simpson.*

The Lord allows, as it were, your trust in Him to be a living pen to write your name on His own Hands in perpetual visibility and remembrance.

Rejoice in the Lord, O ye righteous: for praise is comely for the upright (Psalm 33:1).

> Forbid, O God, that I should lose the song
> That has made me brave and kept me strong
> Through shadowed nights and days o'erlong
> From dawn till setting sun.
>
> For a harried world in quest of gain
> With its dirge of death, its moan of pain,
> Is seeking to still the sweet refrain
> And leave my heart undone.
>
> Yet the song that bears my soul afar
> Through the silver isles of moon and star,
> From the things that seem, to the things that are,
> Is the song of the cross.
>
> A cross of sin and shame that were mine,
> A cross of love, of God's love divine,
> A cross where blood drops like jewels shine,
> Crowning its utter loss.   *E. S. M.*

Ice breaks many a branch, and so I see a great many persons bowed down and crushed by their affliction. But now and then I meet one that sings in affliction, and then I thank God for my own sake as well as his.

There is no such sweet singing as a song in the night.

. . . Christ . . . hath given himself for us an offering and a sacrifice to God for a sweetsmelling savour (Eph. 5:2).

In Sargodha, India, there grows a shrub with exquisite perfume. Sometimes, on summer evenings I had occasion to pass that way. Nothing in the surroundings was attractive, only barrenness and ugliness, mud walls that emitted heat. But when I could get a whiff of this plant's fragrance, I would seem to be cooled and refreshed.

This fragrance is for us to receive and pass on to others. God is ready to make manifest through us the savour of His knowledge in every place we go.

No matter how little natural winsomeness and attractiveness we may have, if we abide in the presence of our Lord, we shall manifest His beauty and His fragrance.

Mary, doubtless, anointed the Lord's feet quietly and inconspicuously, but the house was filled with the odor of the ointment.

Thou hast put gladness in my heart, more than in the time that their corn and their wine increased (Psalm 4:7).

Keep your faith in all beautiful things, though life be gray—in the sun when it is hidden, in the spring when winter reigns. So only will you have the courage to wait for the sure return of brightness and warmth; and to prepare your fields for the coming harvest.

> I find earth not gray, but rosy—
>   Heaven not grim, but fair of hue.
> Do I stoop? I pluck a posy.
>   Do I stand and stare? All's blue.   *Robert Browning.*

No gray day shall darken the sunshine in my soul. No storm shall drench the gladness in my heart.

Produce your cause, said the Lord; bring forth your strong reasons, saith the King of Jacob (Isa. 41:21).

Over in Canada there lived an Irish saint called "Holy Ann." She lived to be one hundred years old. When she was a young girl, she was working in a family for very small wages, under a very cruel master and mistress. They made her carry water for a mile up a steep hill. At one time there had been a well dug there, but it had gone dry; and it stood there year after year.

One night she was very tired, and she fell on her knees and cried to God; while on her knees, she read these words, "I will open . . . fountains in the midst of valleys; I will make the wilderness a pool of water, and the dry land springs of water."

These words struck Holy Ann, and she presented her cause before the Lord. She told Him how badly they needed the water and how hard it was for her to carry the water up the steep hill; then she lay down and fell asleep.

The next morning early she was seen to take a bucket and start for the well. Someone asked her where she was going. She replied, "I am going to draw water from the well."

"Why it is dry," was the answer.

That did not stop Holy Ann. She knew whom she had believed, and on she went; and in the well she found eighty-three feet of pure water! That is the way the Lord can fulfill His promises. "Produce your cause, bring forth your strong reasons," and see Him work in your behalf.

How little we use this method of holy argument in prayer, and yet there are many examples in Scripture: Abraham, Jacob, Moses, Elijah, Daniel—all used arguments in prayer, and *claimed the divine interposition on the ground of the pleas which they presented.*

In this life we have three great lasting qualities—faith, hope and love. But the greatest of them is love (1 Cor. 13:13—Phillips' Trans.).

Faith and hope can see Thy morning star, and love can hear the rustle of a wing.

> In the lone places of my soul
>   The far dim depths, where none can see,
> I hear a little singing bird,
>   For faith has come to live with me.
>
> And o'er the dimness of my way,
>   The vast, gray reaches of my sea,
> There lies a trembling shaft of light,
>   For hope has drifted in to me.
>
> And in this wintry house of mine,
>   Where grief and gloom at home would be,
> A tender hand has lit a fire,
>   For love has come to stay with me.   *Margaret Matthews.*

The key to understanding all God's dealings through the ages is simply a Universal Love going out in redemptive purpose.

. . . Whether we live therefore, or die, we are the Lord's (Rom. 14:8).

It is a wonderful thing to be alive unto God and I believe it is the only way to be kept alive to every good thing that is worth anything . . . We can so live in God that we are in touch with the past, the present, the future. I was thinking yesterday that the most interesting things are those that I have yet to see. The most of my life is before me, because life is not extension, it is satisfaction. Only think, we have never seen His face yet, have never seen our dear ones in their new bodies, and we are to see the coming of Christ, we are to see Him take to Himself His great power, and reign from the rivers to the ends of the earth. All this is before us.

Margaret Bottome.

> In desert wastes I feel no dread,
>   Fearless I walk the trackless sea.
> I care not where my way is led,
>   Since all my life is life with Thee.   *Frank Mason Nash.*

Thou hast set eternity in my heart—how can I tarry with trifles?

Who comforteth us in all our tribulation, that we may be able to comfort them which are in any trouble, by the comfort wherewith we ourselves are comforted of God (2 Cor. 1:4).

S he was a great sufferer too, and daily wrestled with her pitiful disease. But, like the sturdier of the poplars by my gate, she had gathered into herself the force of all the cruel winds that had beaten so savagely upon her. And the result was that her own character had become so strong and so upright and so beautiful . . . that every man and maiden who needed counsel or succour made a beaten path to her open door.

God does not comfort us to make us comfortable, but to make us comforters.

He giveth to his beloved in sleep (Psalm 127:2—RVMargin).

> Turn Thou the key upon our thoughts, dear Lord—
>   And let us sleep;
> Give us our portion of forgetfulness—
>   Silent and deep.
>
> Lay Thou Thy quiet hand upon our eyes,
>   To close their light:
> Shut out the shining of the moon and stars,
>   And candle light.
>
> And lead us far into Thy silent land,
>   That we may go,
> Like children out across the field o' dreams
>   Where poppies blow.
>
> So all Thy saints—and all Thy sinners too—
>   Wilt Thou not keep?
> Since not alone unto the well-beloved
>   Thou givest sleep.   *Virma Shead.*

Can we not learn, like tired children, to fall into the everlasting arms and rest, not in what we know, but in what we trust?

. . . The Lord said unto him, Thou are old and stricken in years, and there remaineth yet very much land to be possessed (Josh. 13:1).

God never throws a man aside because he is old. Joshua was not perhaps as vigorous with the sword as he had been; so God gives him a new bit of work now. He virtually says, "Take the pen and map out the land. There is yet much land to be possessed. Only divide thou it by lot unto the Israelites for an inheritance as I have commanded thee. Now therefore divide this land for an inheritance."

According to our years and strength, God will keep us busy. There is no discharge in this war. We may be old as men, but God would like us to be young and green and fresh at heart.

> Those that within the house of God,
>   Are planted by His grace,
> They shall grow up and flourish all
>   In our God's holy place.
>
> And in old age, when others fade,
>   They fruit still forth shall bring.
> They shall be fat and full of sap,
>   And aye be flourishing.

God will not cast you away. He will not pay you off. There are no superannuates in God's ranks. He will use you and keep you as busy as ever. *Although you may have to come in off the field of battle, although you may have to reduce your outward activities, although you may have to lie upon your bed, God will give you divinely suitable work in your quietly closing years.*

If thy whole body therefore be full of light, having no part dark, the whole shall be full of light, as when the bright shining of a candle doth give thee light (Luke 11:36).

> You're just God's old candle burning out
> And you must burn and not complain
> Till God in His good time blows out the flame.
> We're all God's candles
> And some burn just a little while
> And then are done,
> And others may burn longer and
> There are some
> That burn until the end
> And you are one.
> God knows why
> But to me it seems
> That those whom God allows to burn unto the end
> And give the very last they have to Him
> Are those whom God loves most.
> But anyway—
> You're just God's old candle burning out
> And you must burn and not complain,
> Till God in His good time blows out the flame.

Old candle—let it burn—its light may show a path to someone in the dark.

Make us wise enough to know the flickering candles of our spirits continue their shining only when their wicks are deep in Thy grace.

If then the Spirit of Him, who raised Jesus from the dead, dwells in you, then the Resurrector of Christ Jesus from the dead will through the Spirit that dwells in you make also your mortal bodies alive (Rom. 8:11— Berkeley Version).

Dr. A. B. Simpson who once said that he had lived on the life of another for forty years and would continue to do so until his work was done, wrote that the supernatural secret of Paul's life was that he drew continually in his body from the strength of Christ. "The body which rose from Joseph's tomb was to him a physical reality and the inexhaustible fountain of his vital forces. The Lord is for the body and the body is for the Lord. Marvelous truth! Divine Elixir of life and fountain of perpetual youth. Earnest of the resurrection! Fulfillment of the ancient Psalms and songs of faith. The Lord is the strength of my life, of whom (or what thing) shall I be afraid? My flesh and my heart faint and fail but God is the strength of my heart and my portion forever. Have we learned this secret, and are we living the life of the Incarnate One in our flesh?"

It was Dr. A. J. Gordon who once said, "Does the Holy Spirit take no responsibility in repairing the house in which He lives? If its windows are darkened through infirmity, or its foundations loosened through sickness, must this Divine Tenant remain helpless in His home till some human doctor comes to rectify the evil?"

> Doubt not thy Father's care, doubt not thy Father's care
> For every grief he finds relief and answers every prayer.
> Night comes: the sun is lost;
> Night comes: He doth provide a gleam of a starry host.
>
> All joy is dead, all gladness fled and life has missed its goal.
> Then Thou—the wounded soul in that sad hour
> With wonderous healing power
> Dost touch and makest fully whole.

Mark the perfect man, and behold the upright; for the end of that man is peace (Psalm 37:37).

The Way of Life does not have the end in view. The road winds and what the next step may bring even the anticipating heart knoweth not. I think the best way is just to plod along thoughtfully, prayerfully, lovingly; the end may come in view sometime. That is the way to travel.

Thoughtfully, using the mind; for man may not live by bread alone—and the sustaining reminiscences, anticipations and certitudes are legion and they cheer and safeguard too.

Prayerfully, keeping the soul's vision clear, for the greatest things and the best lie for us in the undeveloped purpose of Him who planned the whole, of which but the half is at present seen.

Lovingly, for when the heart fails, the life is ended; and prayer has its nerve cut; and the mind becomes abject and poor. And love never faileth—whether as chart or clue or prophecy, love keeps faith ever!

> Winds the road drearily, Dear Heart,
>   Love maketh all things new;
> Drags the foot wearily, Dear Heart,
>   The end will come in view.

I see my way, as birds their trackless way . . . He guides me and the birds.

. . . These things saith he that is holy, he that is true, he that hath the key of David, he that openeth, and no man shutteth; and shutteth, and no man openeth (Rev. 3:7).

I t is not at the threshold of life that life reveals its beauty; it is after you have climbed the stairs.

> The day has been long,
> But the hour is now late;
> Weary was the road,
> But at the end is the gate!
>
> Down the dim vista
> Of time that was far,
> Ever the vision
> Of the gate ajar!
>
> Late is the hour
> But morning will break . . .
> Naught but the shining door
> When we awake!
>
> *Lois Snelling.*

God's hand rests upon all gates. He opens the right one at the right time.

Being confident of this very thing, that he which hath begun a good work in you will perform it until the day of Jesus Christ (Phil. 1:6).

A little child was busily engaged in making a toy boat. All day long he worked very hard, trying to finish the boat before the night came. But the boy failed to complete his work, and went away to bed with a feeling of disappointment. When his father came home and saw the unfinished boat, he completed it. Next morning when the lad came down and saw the boat all complete, he said, "I guess the angels must have done it while I was sleeping."

The years come and go so quickly that we shall hardly finish before nightfall.

Finishing is not the important thing, for our little endings may be but larger beginnings.

For we know that if our earthly tabernacle were dissolved, we have a building of God, an house not made with hands, eternal in the heavens (2 Cor. 5:1).

The owner of the tenement which I have occupied for many years has given notice that he will furnish but little or nothing more for repairs. I am advised to be ready to move.

At first this was not a very welcome notice. The surroundings here are in many respects very pleasant, and were it not for the evidence of decay, I should consider the house good enough. But even a light wind causes it to tremble and totter, and all the braces are not sufficient to make it secure. So, I am getting ready to move.

It is strange how quickly one's interest is transferred to the prospective home. I have been consulting maps of the new country and reading descriptions of its inhabitants. One who visited it has returned and from him I learn that it is beautiful beyond description; language breaks down in attempting to tell of what he heard while there. He says that in order to make an investment there, he has suffered the loss of all things that he owned here, and even rejoices in what others would call making a sacrifice. Another, whose love to me has been proven by the greatest possible test, is now there. He has sent me several clusters of the most delicious fruits. After tasting them, all food here seems insipid.

Two or three times I have been down by the border of the river that forms the boundary, and have wished myself among the company of those who were singing praises to the King on the other side. Many of my friends have moved there. Before leaving they spoke of my coming later. I have seen the smile upon their faces as they passed out of sight. *Often I am asked to make some new investments here, but my answer in every case is, "I am getting ready to move."*

. . . I wholly followed the Lord my God (Josh. 14:8).

The Hebrew translation gives a pictorial word describing a ship going at full sail. This was the very keynote of Caleb from beginning to end. He was the man he was from the beginning to the end, because there were no limitations and provisions with him. Having been called by God to His service, he made it his meat and drink. He flung every power of body and soul and spirit like a free sheet to the winds of God's grace, God's spirit and God's providence. There was no hanging back and saving his life and therefore losing it. He did not take just so much of the program because it suited him, scoring out certain items he did not like. He went in for a full program.

With men who give themselves wholly to God, the longer they live, the keener they are. The more difficulties multiply, the more the Lord will gird them with strength. Their strength grows by fighting.

Old age, as a rule, is not sceptical. Old age, as a rule, is believing. Those who have gone farthest, those who have seen the most, those who have traveled along this pilgrim life with various experiences—they are the men who come to have day by day, and year by year, a keener, faster, firmer grip on the unseen and the eternal.

Old men do not turn infidels. Caleb was a grand specimen of a man who entered God's service with all his heart, and found it in the best of all senses to pay—to pay good, sterling, current money's worth.

> He liveth long who liveth well;
>   All else is being flung away.
> He liveth longest who can tell
>   Of true things truly done each day.
> Fill up the hours with what will last;
>   Buy up the moment's as they go,
> The life above, when this is past,
>   Is the ripe fruit of life below.

But now they desire a better country . . . (Heb. 11:16).

Shortly before his death, the Rev. Robert J. Burdette wrote a personal letter to the editor of a paper in which he said:

"I watch the sunset as I look out over the rim of the blue Pacific, and there is no mystery beyond the horizon line, because I know what there is over there. I have been there. I have journeyed in those lands. Over there where the sun is just sinking is Japan. That star is rising over China. In that direction lie the Philippines. I know all that.

"Well, there is another land that I look toward as I watch the sunset. I have never seen it. I have never seen anyone who has been there. But it has a more abiding reality than any of those lands which I do know.

"This land is beyond the sunset—this land of immortality, this fair and blessed country of the soul—why, this heaven of ours is the one thing in the world which I know with absolute, unshaken, unchangeable certainty. This I know with a knowledge that is never shadowed by a passing cloud of doubt. I may not always be certain about this world; my geographical locations may sometimes become confused, but the other world—that I know.

"And as the afternoon sun sinks lower, faith shines more clearly and hope, lifting her voice in a higher key, sings the songs of fruition. My work is about ended, I think. The best of it I have done poorly; any of it I might have done better, but I have done it. *And in the fairer land, with finer materials and a better working light, I will do better work.*"

. . . *The Lord is thy shade upon thy right hand (Psalm 121:5).*

The kindliest thing God ever made
His hand of very healing laid
Upon a fevered world, is shade.

His glorious company of trees
Throw out their mantles, and on these
The dust-stained wanderer finds ease.

Green temples, closed against the beat
Of noontimes's blinding glare and heat
Open to any pilgrim's feet.

The white road blisters in the sun;
Now, half the weary journey done,
Enter and rest, oh, weary one!

And feel the dew of dawn still wet
Beneath thy feet and so forget
The burning highway's ache and fret.

This is God's hospitality,
And whoso rests beneath a tree
Hath cause to thank Him gratefully.   *T. Harrison.*

What is my cloud, after all—shade of His hand outstretched caressingly.

Thou shalt come to thy grave in a full age, like as a shock of corn cometh in, in his season (Job 5:26).

Can you believe that God gave to man the gift of life, meaning the first half of it to be the best?

Can you believe that it is His purpose that the most hopeless part of life should be the end? There are, it is true, links with the material world that men shed as they grow older, but these are of the husks of life and not the kernel.

Maturity of mind is a greater thing than maturity of body and comes later. Maturity of soul, the greatest thing of all, does not seem to come here at all. Souls are still growing when they leave the lower school. This is surely not "going downhill." That is surely what God means life to be for all of us—a road that leads "uphill all the way."

> Weary traveler! traveling onward
>   Traveling onward toward the goal,
> Let the star of hope enlighten
>   Lighten up thy fainting soul;
> Though night's gloomy shades are falling,
>   Falling round thee dark and drear,
> Do thou with faith, still progress onward,
>   Onward march and never fear!

So far in the history of the world there have never been enough mature people in the right places.

My soul melteth for heaviness: strengthen thou me according unto thy word (Psalm 119:28).

He who looks alone at the enemy at hand has no song, but only the pitiful lament of that unknown colored man who gives us a new type of Negro blues:

Jis blue, God, jis blue,
Ain't praying exactly jis now
Tear blind I guess
Can't see my way through
You know those things I ast for so many times
Maybe I hadn't orter repeat like the Pharisees do;
But I ain't stood in no market place
It's jis between me and you.
    And you said "ast."
    Somehow I ain't astin' now
    And I hardly know what to do.

Hope jis sorter left—
But faith still here
Faith ain't gone too
    I know now 'tis.
    A thousand years
Is a single day to you
And I ain't meanin' to tempt you with "If you be . . . "
And I ain't doubtin' you
But I ain't prayin' Lord,
    Jis blue.

When life grows sore and wounding and it is difficult to be brave, begin by praising. Sing something and you will rally your own heart with the song.

Do not depend upon frames and feelings. You cannot always live in the tropics.

Bear ye one another's burdens, and so fulfill the law of Christ (Gal. 6:2).

> In every patch of timber you
> Will always find a tree or two
> That would have fallen long ago,
> Borne down by wind or age or snow,
> Had not another neighbor tree
> Held out its arms in sympathy
> And caught the tree that the storm had hurled
> To earth. So, neighbors, is the world.
> In every patch of timber stand
> Samaritans of forest land,
> The birch, the maple, oak and pine,
> The fir, the cedar, all in line!
> In every wood unseen, unknown,
> They bear their burdens of their own
> And bear as well another form,
> Some neighbor stricken in the storm.
> Shall trees be nobler to their kind
> Than men, who boast the noble mind;
> Shall there exist within the wood
> This great eternal brotherhood
> Of oak and pine, of hill and fen,
> And not within the hearts of men?
> God grant that men are like to these,
> And brothers, brotherly as trees.

I am more than my brother's keeper—I am my brother's brother.

For every house is builded by some man; but he that built all things is God. (Heb. 3:4).

This world is but a quarry where the living stones of the Heavenly Jerusalem are cut and molded.

What is anything when you think of eternity, except a means to get there—so laugh at everything and go on in His Name.

> What matters it to us who are immortal
> Which side of the grave we stand on, when we know
> That what the world calls death is but the portal
> Leading to life again? 'Tis but to go
> Across the gurgling river in the dark
> Hanging on God; and but a moment so
> Till we are over, and we disembark
> And enter life afresh. 'Tis basely wrong
> We should so meanly understrike the mark
> As measures life by years; and all long
> Busy ourselves arranging little schemes
> That death will dash to pieces, when we might
> Be building, far above those earthly dreams,
> Houses that stand forever in God's sight.

He who would pass the latter part of his days with honor and decency must when he is young, consider that he shall one day be old; and remember when he is old that he once was young.

I will bless the Lord at all times . . . (Psalm 34:1).

Continue in prayer and watch in the same with thanksgiving (Col. 4:2).

The twin keys that unlock the doors to His treasure chest: Praise and prayer! Keys that open the windows of heaven and let the showers of heaven descend! Oh, the power of prayer and praise! It can open every prison door and set the prisoners free.

What it did for Peter and Paul and Silas it can do for us no matter where that confinement may be. Show me a more wretched captive than a worrying Christian whose song has been stilled by Satan. The song of praise and the voice of prayer would open the prison for him, even though it might be midnight in the soul.

To the natural man, "In nothing be anxious; but in everything by prayer and supplication with thanksgiving," may seem an impossible injunction. But the Christian deals with the supernatural!

In the Lord's care—in the grasp of His love, all is safe, all is utterly safe.

. . . I am the light of the world; he that followeth me shall not walk in darkness . . . (John 8:12).

> Into the dark, Lord Jesus,
> Into the dark with Thee,
> There hath come to my heart a calling apart,
> And a whispered, "Follow Me."
>
> Take Thou my hand, Lord Jesus,
> In Thy mighty clasp divine;
> Hold it so close, Lord Jesus,
> That it tremble not in Thine;
> For my heart shrinks back from the unknown track,
> And my feet tread falteringly;
> And into the dark I follow—
> Into the dark with Thee.
>
> Into the dark, Lord Jesus,
> Is it the dark with Thee?
> Nay, Thou makest the night about me light,
> And mine eyes—mine eyes shall see—
> Shall "see the King in His beauty,"
> In the land that is far away;
> Shall see in the heavenly sunshine,
> The path that is hid today.
>
> Then why should I fear what the untried year
> May bring to mine or me?
> Into the dark I follow—
> Nay, into the Light, with Thee!   *Edith Gilling Cherry.*

Deep sorrows sometimes prove to be God's masked mercies. The worst sorrows in life are not its losses, and misfortunes, but its fears.

. . . The valley of the shadow . . . (Psalm 23:4).

Methinks I see that valley now. The shepherd is conducting his flock toward their fold: luxuriant pastures; quiet resting-places.

Suddenly that path turns downward and beings to wind toward the ravine below. On the one side is a precipice, yawning in sheer descent to the steep river-bed, where the water foams and roars, torn by jagged rocks. On the other side, the mountain firs cast a somber shadow in the deepening twilight. It would be dark there in the most brilliant noon.

Such is the valley through which the great Shepherd once went alone; by which He now conducts all His flock to their home.

Death is not an abiding-place. It is a valley through which we walk. Darksome, lonely, infested with evil things; but we do not pitch our tents there. We pass through it to our rest!

. . . He shall go no more out . . . (Rev. 3:12).

> The day dies slowly in the western sky;
>   The sunset splendor fades, and wan and cold
> The far peaks wait the sunrise; cheerily
>   The goat-herd calls his wanderers to the fold.
>
> My weary soul, that fain would cease to roam,
>   Take comfort; evening bringeth all things home.
> Homeward the swift-winged sea-gull takes her flight;
>   The ebbing tide breaks softer on the sand;
>
> The red-sailed boats draw shoreward for the night,
>   The shadows deepen over sea and land.
> Be still my soul, thine hour shall also come;
>   Behold, one evening, God shall lead thee home.

Evening brings us homeward to our Father's House.

For I am already being poured out as a drink-offering, and the time of my setting sail is near (2 Tim. 4:6—Berkeley Version).

How beautiful it is so to live that the lamp of life is trimmed and burning when the Bridegroom comes, so that the sail is spread when the gales of heaven blow, so that the sheaf is ripe when the reapers arrive, and so that the fruit is mellow when the day of vintage comes.

And when the sands of life are almost run; when life's golden day is ebbing to its close; when the twilight of time is melting into the twilight of eternity, whose glory shall increase to an eternal summer noon, then with the Poet Laureate of the Victorian Age, may you be able to sing:

> Sunset and evening star
>   And one clear call for me,
> And may there be no moaning of the bar
>   When I put out to sea.
>
> But such a tide as moving seems asleep,
>   Too full for sound and foam,
> When that which drew from out the boundless deep,
>   Turns again home.
>
> Twilight and evening bell,
>   And after that the dark!
> And may there be no sadness of farewell,
>   When I embark;
>
> For tho' from out our bourne of time and place
>   The flood may bear me far,
> I hope to see my Pilot face to face
>   When I have crossed the bar.

The pilgrim they laid in a large upper chamber facing the sunrising and the name of that chamber was peace.

. . . When I am old and gray-headed, O God, forsake me not; until I have shown thy strength unto this generation . . . (Psalm 71:18).

There may still await aged and trembling some important task.

Lord when Thou seest that my work is done,
Let me not linger on,
With failing powers,
Adown the weary hours,
A workless worker in a world of work.
But with a word,
Just bid me home,
And I will come
Right gladly,
Yea, right gladly
Will I come.   *John Oxenham.*

Lord, let me not live to be useless! (John Wesley's Prayer).

Who is among you that feareth the Lord, that obeyeth the voice of his servant, that walketh in darkness and hath no light? let him trust in the name of the Lord and stay upon his God (Isa. 50:10).

Look diligently for that treasure of your experience of the Grace of God toward you.

Have you never a Hill Mizar to remember? Have you forgotten the milk house, the stable, the barn, and the like, where God did visit your souls? Remember, I say, the word upon which the Lord caused you to hope.

Never had I in all my life so great an inlet into the Word of God as now (in Bedford Jail); those Scriptures that I saw nothing in before, are made in this place and state to shine before me; Jesus Christ also was never more real and apparent than now; here I have seen and felt Him indeed.   *John Bunyan.*

> He cannot heal who has not suffered much
> For only sorrow, sorrow understands;
> They will not come for healing at our touch
> Who have not see the scars upon our hands.   *E. P.*

. . . I will do better unto you than at your beginnings; and ye shall know that I am the Lord (Ezek. 36:11).

There is a power in ripe and chastened old age which transcends that of any ordinary period of life. On such hoary heads, the hands of God himself have been laid with a consecrating touch which sets them apart, though never aloof, from their fellows.

> God keep my heart attuned to laughter
>   When youth is done;
> When all the days are gray days, coming after
>   The warmth, the sun.
> God keep me then from bitterness, from grieving,
>   When life seems cold.
> God keep me always loving and believing
>   As I grow old.

Blessed is the man or woman who so live that they enjoy tarrying in the house of old age.

For even hereunto were ye called: because Christ also suffered for us, leaving us an example, that ye should follow his steps (1 Peter 2:21).

> How nice it was of You to be
>   A little child, dear God.
> I love to think my feet are on
>   The same world that you trod.   *Mary Dixon Thayer.*

I have loved to hear my Lord spoken of; and wherever I have seen the print of His shoe in the earth, there have I coveted to set my foot also.

> The Carpenter of Galilee
> Comes down the street again,
> In every land, in every age,
> He still is building men.
> On Christmas Eve we hear Him knock;
> He goes from door to door:
> "Are any workmen out of work?
> The Carpenter needs more."   *H. W. S.*

Lord, now lettest thou thy servant depart in peace, according to thy word: for mine eyes have seen thy salvation (Luke 2:29, 30).

S imeon waited for the Messiah, and knew that he had not waited in vain. Scientists tell us that the flowers of the Alps buried for long months under the snow are yet full of energy and expectation, and no sooner does the sun shine than in a few hours they open into glorious flowers.

So aged Simeon waited through a long life, waited buried under the cold snows, but at the first kiss of the Sun of Righteousness he broke into flower and blossomed as the rose.

A smile of encouragement at the right moment may act like sunlight on a closed-up flower—it may be the turning point for a struggling life.

. . . We have seen his star in the east, and are come to worship him (Matt. 2:2).

> Men travel bravely by a thousand roads,
> Some broad and lined with palaces; some steep
> And hard and lonely, some that blindly twist
> Through tangled jungles where there is no light;
> And mostly they are traveled thoughtlessly.
> But once a year an ancient question comes
> To every traveler passing on his way,
> A question that can stab and burn and bless.
> "Is this the road that leads to Bethlehem?"

Dare to follow the star-blazed road.

*They sat in darkness and in the shadow of death . . . (Psalm 107:10—
Modern Trans.).*

The Day-Spring from on high hath visited us (Luke 1:78).

*Now when Jesus was born in Bethlehem . . . (Matt. 2:1 Psalm 107:10—
Modern Trans.).*

What? The morning dawned upon that night-burdened, shadow-haunted, fear-filled world. "The Dayspring"— could anything be more appropriate to the fearful hearts of the tenants of the night? Not the full day, but the spring of the day, the light fountain.

When Jesus was born in Bethlehem, He dawned upon the world as a Carpenter. He beamed upon the night realms in the soft warm rays of a summer's morn. He came as the day-spring, the opening fountain of the day, the first little spring which is to issue at last in the immeasurable glory of Eternal light and truth.

Dr. Jowett.

May Christ Himself, through us, enter again into this world of darkness.

For unto you is born this day in the city of David a Saviour, which is Christ the Lord (Luke 2:11).

> Men scoff at miracles. "They cannot be," they say;
> "Christ was not born of Mary; there could be no virgin birth.
> 'Tis but a lovely legend of the Godhead come to earth.
> And yet, I heard the bells of Bethlehem, ring out this Christmas Day,
> And the clangor of their ringing was ten thousand miles away.

The meaning of Christmas is Immanuel—God with us, the Word becoming flesh. Just as one can analyze the tiny sunbeam and discover in it the chemical make-up of the vast sun, so I look at Jesus Christ's life and know what God is like. A little boy expressed the miracle of the incarnation thus, "Jesus is the nicest picture God ever had made."

The Christian spirit is the Christmas spirit, extended through the whole year—it is an attitude toward every person, the atmosphere of every act.

> Then let every heart keep its Christmas within,
> Christ's pity for sorrow, Christ's hatred for sin.
> Christ's care for the weakest, Christ's courage for right.
> Christ's dread of the darkness, Christ's love of the light;
> Everywhere, everywhere, Christmas tonight.

. . . Go and show John again those things which ye do hear and see; the blind receive their sight, and the lame walk . . . and the deaf hear . . . (Matt. 11:4, 5).

There's a beautiful legend, that's never been told,
It may have been known to the wise men of old—
How three little children came early at dawn,
With hearts that were sad, to where Jesus was born.
One could not see, one was too lame to play;
While the other, a mute, not a word could he say.

Yet led by His star, they came there to peep
At the little Lord Jesus, with eyes closed in sleep.
But how could the Christ child, so lovely and fair,
Not waken and smile when He heard their glad prayer,

Of hope at His coming, of faith in His birth,
Of praise at His bringing God's peace to the earth.
And then as the light softly came through the door,
The lad that was lame stood upright once more;
The boy that was mute started sweetly to sing,
While the child that was blind looked with joy on the
King!   *Charles W. H. Bancroft.*

There will always be a Christmas, and it will always bring new hope, new courage—as always through the darkness the Christmas star shines its pledge of peace and freedom.

. . . Be ye steadfast, unmoveable, always abounding in the work of the Lord, forasmuch as ye know that your labor is not in vain in the Lord (1 Cor. 15:58).

One of the finest sights in the world is a Christian at the end of a long course with an unsullied reputation. His hair may be white, but his leaf is green. Such a one was Whittier, America's great Quaker poet. With, surely, a singular appropriateness, he bore the name John Greenleaf Whittier. Though many years have gone since his labors ceased on earth, his works do follow him. Countless hearts, in every clime today, are comforted and cheered by the fragrant messages which poured forth from his full and fruitful life, a life which had its roots fixed firmly in God and in His Word. Very sweetly has he expressed the secret of his fertility in the following lines:

> The same old baffling questions; O, my friend,
> I cannot answer them.
>
> I have no answer for myself or thee,
> Save that I learned beside my mother's knee;
> "All is of God that is, and is to be;
> And God is good." Let this suffice us still,
> Resting in childlike trust upon His will
> Who moves to His great ends unthwarted by the ill.

In old age we rest again in simple truth and trust, only with a fuller inward witness and more spiritual calm—and so the evening light is as the morning's and sheds once more the tenderest beauty on the world.

. . . God was in Christ, reconciling the world unto himself . . . (2 Cor. 5:19).

There is on record a story of how a tribe of North American Indians who roamed in the neighbourhood of Niagara, offered year by year a young virgin as a sacrifice to the Spirit of the Mighty River. She was called "The Bride of the Falls."

The lot fell one year on a beautiful girl who was the only daughter of an old chieftain. The news was carried to him while he was sitting in his tent; but on hearing it, the old man went on smoking his pipe and said nothing of what he felt.

On the day fixed for the sacrifice, a white canoe, full of ripe fruits, and decked with beautiful flowers, was ready, waiting to receive the bride.

At the appointed hour she took her place in the frail bark, which was pushed out into mid-stream, where it would be carried swiftly toward the mighty cataract.

Then, to the amazement of the crowd which had assembled to watch the sacrifice, a second canoe was seen to dart out from the river's bank a little lower down the stream. In it was seated the old chieftain.

With swift strokes he paddled toward the canoe in which was his beloved child, and on reaching it, he gripped it firmly and held it fast.

The eyes of both met in one last long look of love; and then, close together, father and daughter were carried by the racing current until they plunged over the thundering cataract and perished side by side.

In their death they were not divided; the father was in it with his child!

"God was in Christ, reconciling the world unto himself." He did not have to. Nobody forced Him. *The only force behind that sacrifice was the force of His seeking love for a lost world.*

. . . Rooted and grounded in love (Eph. 3:17).

Not long ago I watched a great tree bend before a gale. The storm passed on; then it returned in renewed fury. Would the tree, which had weathered the winds of many summers and the blasts of many winters, stand in this, the worst gale in the memory of the oldest resident? Eagerly I watched, for the tree had come to be a symbol of strength. The wind wearied and ceased. Slowly the tree righted itself. The sun shone on its green crown, greener and more beautiful than before, for the rain had washed away the dust of many weeks.

What held the tree as it bowed before the storm? Ah, the taproot was down deep in the earth; the other roots gripped firmly for a distance of many feet. The tree was securely anchored. The gales of its life had only caused the roots to go deeper, to draw more nourishment from the ground in which it stood.

Then I thought how like this tree our lives may be if we are "rooted and grounded" in the immeasurable love of God. Troubles may come, but they will not overwhelm us. Grief may shut out the sunshine for a time, but it will make our lives the more beautiful if only we allow it to do so.

The hardiest trees are not reared in hot-houses, but where they can battle with wind and tempest; "moored in the rifted rock."

Cast me not off in the time of old age; forsake me not when my strength faileth (Psalm 71:9).

Years are not the measure of one's age. We ought to be calmer as we grow older, if not happier, knowing better what life is and looking forward to another which is reality, even though we cannot tell what it will be like.

> Gone they tell me is youth,
> Gone is the strength of my life,
> Nothing remains but decline,
> Nothing but age and decay.
>
> Not so, I'm God's little child,
> Only beginning to live;
> Coming the years of my prime,
> Coming the strength of my life,
> Coming the vision of God,
> Coming my bloom and my power.

Make the best of age—not the best of what is bad at the best, but of what is the best of your life, because it is the last.

Grow old along with me—the best is yet to be!

. . . There hath not failed one word of all his good promise, which he promised by the hand of Moses his servant (1 Kings 8:56).

A late lark twitters from the quiet skies,
And from the west,
Where the sun, his day's work ended
Lingers as in content,
There falls on the old gray city
An influence luminous and serene,
A shining peace.

The smoke ascends
In a rosy-and-golden haze. The spires
Shine and are changed. In the valley
Shadows rise. The lark sings on. The sun,
Closing his benediction,
Sinks and the darkening air
Thrills with a sense of the triumphing night—
Night with her train of stars
And her great gift of sleep.

So be my passing!
My task accomplished and the long day done,
My wages taken and in my heart
Some late lark singing,
Let me be gathered to the quiet west
The sundown splendid and serene.

My sword I give to him that shall succeed me in my pilgrimage; and my courage and skill to him that can get it; my marks and scars I carry with me to be a witness that I have fought his battles, Who now will be my rewarder.   *John Bunyan.*

"Now the God of peace, that brought again from the dead our Lord Jesus, that great shepherd of the sheep, through the blood of the everlasting covenant, make you perfect in every good work to do his will, working in you that which is wellpleasing in his sight, through Jesus Christ; to whom be glory for ever and ever "(Heb. 13:20, 21).

The Lord bless thee and keep thee:
The Lord make his face shine upon thee
And be gracious unto thee:
The Lord lift up his countenance upon thee
    And give thee peace.   *(Numbers 6:24-26).*

ACKNOWLEDGMENTS

The compiler takes pleasure in acknowledging the kindness of authors and publishers who very generously have granted permission to use extracts from their copyrighted publications.

Among those to whom such acknowledgments are due, I list the following: Abingdon-Cokesbury Press of Nashville, Tennessee, for permission to quote "I Love a Tree" from *Hilltop Verses and Prayers* by Bishop Ralph S. Cushman; The Broadman Press of Nashville, Tennessee, for permission to quote "We Must Go On" from *I Shall Meet Tomorrow Bravely* by Sybil Leonard Armes; Christian Publications, Inc., of Harrisburg, Pennsylvania, for permission to quote from the writings of Dr. A. B. Simpson; Harper and Brothers for permission to quote from *The Bible a New Translation* by James Moffatt, for permission to quote "New Year" by Thomas Wearing, "Per Pacem et Lucem" by Adelaide Procter, and "Shade" by T. Garrison from *Masterpieces of Religious Verse,* and for permission to quote "After Work" by John Oxenham from *Selected Poems of John Oxenham*; Robert G. Lee of Bellevue Baptist Church, Memphis, Tennessee, for permission to quote from his writings; The Macmillan Company, Publishers, of New York, for permission to quote from *Letters to Young Churches* by J. B. Phillips; Roy L. Smith of the Methodist Publishing House for permission to quote from his writings; Zondervan Publishing House of Grand Rapids, Michigan, for permission to quote from *The Berkeley Version of the New Testament* by Gerrit Verkuyl.

An earnest endeavor has been made to locate the authors of all copyrighted selections; indulgence is begged where this endeavor has failed. Should we succeed in locating any further copyright owners, acknowledgment will be given in the next edition.